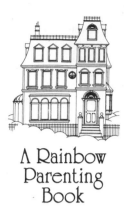

Λ Rainbow
Parenting
Book

Praise for *Learning Disabilities 101*

"Mary Cathryn has given a gift to all families forced to deal with a learning disability. As Danny's uncle, I have watched him grow and prosper in a loving, caring family. Now, Mary Cathryn has shared her experience for other families to learn. She articulates everything a family must expect, but makes clear why they should never lose hope. I admire her courage and urge all parents to read this important book."
— U.S. Representative (FL) Dan Miller

"As the parent of a learning disabled child and as a legislator who deals with the issue on a day to day basis, I thought I was thoroughly familiar with the subject. I was wrong. Mary Cathryn Haller has written an important book for all of us — not just those with learning disabled children. It takes a subject that is all too often obscured with professional jargon and offers clear, concise, and wise advice for both parents and professionals."
— Florida State Senator John McKay

"As a Special Educator, Psychologist, Administrator and parent, I have a variety of experiences in working with learning disabled children. From these different vantage points, I realize the importance of a parent's role in shaping the life of a child. It is a parent's love and understanding that develops a child's self-esteem and it is the development of this self-esteem that impacts a learning disabled child's ability to meet and conquer the many challenges that he may encounter. These pages are filled with the knowledge and understanding that a parent needs to accomplish these tasks. Mary Cathryn Haller provides parents with the tools needed to guide and support our children through the challenges and obstacles of handling these disabilities. This book is a must read for parents and educators as we dedicate ourselves to the pursuance of happiness and success for our children."
— Patricia L. Knight, Director of Academic Support
Phelps School, Malvern, PA

"As a professional who has so often found myself struggling for the most supportive way to 'break the news' to a parent of a child with learning disabilities, I see this book as a positive breakthrough in assisting parents. Parents of children and young adults with learning problems experience stressful highs and lows in their efforts to understand the issues and advocate properly. The information in this book will help parents feel competent in the quest to help their children maximize their potentials."

— Sister M. Gilchrist Cottrill, SND

"As an evaluation specialist, I would recommend this book to parents just entering the evaluation stage of their child's educational assessment or for those trying to make sense of what they have just been through. It is written in layman's terms and easy for a noneducator to understand. Its format gives plenty of practical information without overwhelming the parent."

— Susan M. Kelly, M.A.
The Educational Evaluation Center, Bradenton, FL

"As the parent of a special needs student, Mary Cathryn Haller brings a unique sensitivity to this book. With her boundless energy and the ability to look at the bright side of every situation, she organizes years of her own research into a must read book for parents of children diagnosed with learning disabilities."

— Judith Edwards, Director
Oakland School, Boyd's Tavern, VA

"This book is valuable in that it is written simply but reflects and expresses a depth of emotional realization over a lifetime of experiences with a child who has special needs. It refrains from the usual professional 'jargon,' which will inspire parents looking for answers . . . Professionals along the way have to be those in a posture to reflect the information needed to support parents as they search for help. It is a highly personal time. The journey . . . becomes one of seeking professionals who have learned to respect parents who know their children best and will listen to words of wisdom, ask questions sensitively, and offer solutions that will truly make a difference. Once this balance is achieved between parents and professionals through understanding and mutual respect, most of what children with disabilities need can be accomplished. The work is never easy or completed, but the best situations for children are usually the ones that are processed by people who can work creatively together to make solutions an option (rather than discussing the obstacles). This book is a win-win for parents and their children as well as professionals who have learned how to effectively help."

— Louise Boothby, Ph.D., Child Development Specialist, Div. of Child Development and Neurology, Dept. of Pediatrics, College of Medicine, Univ. of South Florida

"This book is an excellent resource for parents as well as for the learning disabled adolescent . . . easy to read and understand. . . . written in non-technical language and gives parents knowledge and understanding of the real life challenges of having a child with a learning disability. . . . I highly recommend this book for parents who are involved in the initial diagnosis process for learning disabilities, as well as parents already dealing with the life challenges of having a child with learning disabilities."

— Belinda S. Strickland, Special Education Teacher (23 years)
Alexandria, VA

Learning Disabilities 101

A Primer for Parents

Written by a Parent
for Parents of Children
with Learning Disabilities

Mary Cathryn Haller

Library of Congress Cataloging-in-Publication Data

Haller, Mary Cathryn.
    Learning disabilities 101 : a primer for parents / Mary Cathryn Haller.
      p.   cm.
    Includes bibliographical references.
    ISBN 1-56825-073-8 (acid-free paper)
      1. Learning disabled children--Education--United States.
    2. Learning disabilities--United States. 3. Eduation--Parent participation-
-United States. I. Title. II. Title: Learning disabilities one hundred one.
III. Title: Learning disabilities one hundred and one.
    LC4705.H36   1999
    371.9--dc21   98-44036
                                                             CIP

Learning Disabilities 101
A Primer for Parents
by Mary Cathryn Haller

All inquiries (as well as library/retail/wholesale/distributor/STOP orders/
media requests) should be addressed to:

Rainbow Books, Inc.
P.O. Box 430
Highland City, FL 33846-0430
Editorial Offices:
        Order and Media Contact Telephone: (888) 613-BOOK (2665)
        Fax: (941) 648-4420
        Email: RBIbooks@aol.com

Individual Orders: (800) 356-9315, Fax (800) 242-0036

Cover and Interior Design: Betsy Lampé

Printed in the United States of America.

To the men in my life
Greg, Chris, and Dan
All my love

Contents

Foreword

This book meets the needs of millions of parents who have been informed that their son or daughter has a learning disability. This diagnosis usually comes from a pediatrician, school counselor, psychologist, learning specialist or special education teacher. When parents first hear the words "learning disability", they do not understand what it means or how it affects their child. The professionals who give them this information are talking in their professional vernacular, which most parents do not understand. If the parents are advised to read reference materials, such as books and journal articles, they rarely understand that information. Even if the parents do understand the book and journal articles, it is very difficult to generalize the information to their child. The hundreds of questions parents have cannot be answered by these references, which results in even more frustration.

This book will explain in layman's terms how a learning disability affects your child and what you can do about it. Even with support from your school counselor or special education instructor you will still need this informative book to talk to them in their language and understand what they tell you.

This book should be the first book you read on learning disabilities because it will help you understand the other books you will read on learning disabilities. If you already have books or journal articles on learning disabilities, you will need this book to help you interpret them. The audience for this book is any relative of or friend to a child with a learning disability.

The first step to helping your child is to know how learning disabilities affect your child's learning. As you may know, there are various types of learning disabilities which are all different. You need to understand and accept your child's specific learning disability and recognize his/her learning strengths and weaknesses. Mrs. Haller discusses this information from a parent-to-parent perspective in the first two chapters.

Understanding the law and knowing your rights and your child's rights are the next important steps in helping your child. In Chapter 3, Mrs. Haller talks you through the laws – in understandable terms – from the viewpoint of a parent. She also explains how to apply the law when writing an IEP.

The role of the family and how a learning disability affects the family is rarely written about in a book on learning disabilities. In Chapter 4, Mrs. Haller demonstrates her insight as the mother of a child with a learning disability, and she describes how the family can be preserved intact. Chapter 5 discusses the different types of psychoeducational tests, which most parents cannot understand; Ms. Haller explains these tests in terms parents can understand. She offers the same clear explanations in the chapter covering ADD and ADHD, two disorders which are known to occur in some children with learning disabilities.

Mrs. Haller really breaks new ground in Chapters 7, 8 and 9. From a parent's point of view she examines school options — public, private and homeschooling. Other books on learning disabilities do not make these comparisons.

Finally, Mrs. Haller gives you her personal tips for managing both your child with a learning disability and your household. These tips are from her own experiences and will be very valuable to you.

This is the best book for parents to understand how to help their child with a learning disability. Its parent-to-parent perspective and insights make it a book the entire family can use.

—Paul Nolting, Ph.D.
Learning Specialist,
Mental Health Counselor (MH-419)
and author of
Math and the Learning Disabled Student
and *Winning at Math*

Acknowledgments

Never in my wildest dreams would I have thought I would someday write a book, not to mention a book inspired by my son, Dan. But they say in the business that you should write your first book on something that you really, really know. Dan is 19 now, and trust me when I say, "I really, really know about learning disabilities" — at least from a parent's point of view — because Dan is a child with learning disabilities. But I must say, I wish I had written this book much sooner, as not only do I think it is a beneficial book for all parents of children with learning disabilities (as well as professionals), but it was also therapeutic for me to write on this topic.

There were so many of my friends who not only encouraged me to write this book but who continued that encouragement throughout its writing that I cannot begin to thank them enough. First of all, I want to thank Debbie Dye, who was the brainchild behind this book and even helped edit several of the chapters. I also want to thank my in-laws, Bob and Maxine Haller, my dear sister-in-law Debbie, my niece Susan, and my former professors Dr. Louise Boothby and Brenda Watkins, who generously gave their time to review and comment on early drafts of this book. Their advice and suggestions were well-heeded. A particular thanks to Nan Sizemore, a terrific English teacher who did a superb job editing the entire book. (I wish she had taught me grammar in high school!)

And I want to thank my friends – the Manatee River Queens (Kathy, Belinda and Sara), The Fab Five (Derek, Virginia, Melitta and Nancy in spirit), my Colorado friends: Gayle, Mara, Mimi and Ruth, and my Florida friends: Carol, Kris and Brian, Janis, Cristina and Julie – your encouragement and enthusiasm, humor and laughter (laughter is the best medicine) kept me going when I could not write any more.

And to my friend and my collaborator for my next book, Solveig Peters, who enthusiastically encouraged the completion of this book. A special thanks to Dr. Paul Nolting, an author many times over and an expert in the field of Learning Disabilities, who did an outstanding job editing and verifying my research and then offering to write the Foreword. And with special appreciation, I thank my husband, Greg, and my sons, Chris and Dan, for their patience and support while I worked overtime to complete this book and to whom I dedicate this book.

I would like to acknowledge the Washington State Superintendent of Public Instruction, Special Education Section, for allowing us to use its report on Section 504, *Meeting the Needs of All Students: Section 504 of the Rehabilitation Act of 1973*. This document was developed in cooperation with Region 10 of the Office for Civil Rights.

Introduction

This book is a primer – the first book that parents, grandparents, aunts and uncles should read when they learn their child, grandchild, niece or nephew is diagnosed learning disabled (LD). As a parent of a child with learning disabilities, I worked through the maze of technical terms, laws and problems without the benefit of a "how-to" book, and that is one reason why I wrote this book.

I wrote this book in understandable language because I have attended too many conferences with the "experts" who used only technical and medical terminology. In the beginning, I was so intimidated, I did not stop them in their tracks; rather, I agreed with whatever they were saying so that I did not (for heaven's sake) look dumb or foolish. Does all this sound too familiar?

I chose to write this guide for the parents of children

with LD so they could learn from my mistakes. When I first held my son in my arms and looked him in the eyes, I did not see "LD" written across his forehead. What I saw was a beautiful, healthy baby boy who could grow up to be even President of the United States!

As Dan grew, so did his disability. By age two, it was evident something was not right. But how many of you have heard "Oh, he will outgrow it", or "Your uncle was always a little slow", or "Don't worry, he's just a boy"? Have you heard anything like that before?

So I had to learn the hard way, by trial and error, and believe me, I made my share of errors. The most blatant and probably the most unforgiving error that I made in my son's education was to believe in the public school "system". I was an educated mother with both a Bachelor's degree and a Master's in Education! I was a former teacher and a successful businesswoman. When I was a teacher, I thought I was one of the best. In fact, in anything I pursued I gave it my all. Failure was not something that I seriously considered as possible. When I came upon a problem in life, I always checked the sources, read what I could, and, as often as possible, consulted the so-called "experts" and then made the decision. In the past, that process worked in the educational world as well as the business world. But when it came to parenting – you started from scratch. I believe any parent will tell you there are no "experts". Unfortunately, when it came to my son's schooling, I believed the "experts" – the schools, the teachers, the educators – the professionals!

Fortunately, by my son's 10th birthday, I realized my mistakes and started advocating on his behalf and not relying on the "system". Once I took charge of my son's education, asking questions and probing the experts, I realized that I did not have to *rely* on what the so-called "system" threw at me, and, furthermore, I was not *intimated* by all the so-called "experts". I even increased my vocabulary so I could speak in the same language as the professionals!

This book helps parents of children with LD understand the basic language and terms, know how to find the experts and professionals, and to be able to recognize their options. This book, written in "parent" language, will help parents understand three things: how to cope with their child's disability, how to work through a maze of laws and medical terms and how the family fits into their child's LD world.

This "survival guide" will give parents school options, teach parents their rights under the law (without attending law school), and show parents how to contact and form local, state and national support groups. Other practical information includes what records to keep and the importance of self-esteem and social development for the child with LD. Other areas addressed include testing, an understanding of why those tests should be used and basic information on Attention Deficit Hyperactivity Disorder (ADHD). The last chapter is a "nuts and bolts" survival chapter to help parents work with their child with LD. It is a refresher course that can rejuvenate the very busy parent who is totally overwhelmed parenting a child with LD. At the end of each chapter are both a summary and a list of frequently asked questions, with answers. The Suggested Reading list at the end of this book, broken down by chapter, includes books, periodicals and websites which are geared to the parent. The Bibliography includes the professional-level volumes to which I refer in this text. Basically, I want to share with parents what I had to learn the hard way!

In order for you and your child to survive in the "un-LD" world (a world geared to the regular folks), education is the key – parents must continually research and study everything they can on LD, and, in particular, zero in on their child's particular LD learning problem. You cannot rely on just what the professionals and experts you encounter will tell you. You must understand the extent of your child's LD so that you can work together *with* the professionals — educators, medical doctors, school systems — to advocate (argue, plead or recommend) for your child and to teach your child how to advocate when mature enough to do so. This survival guide will help you do just that.

Working through the maze of terms, laws and problems is not a bed of roses. But when you realize you are working *on behalf of your child*, what more rewarding adventure could you want?

Let me now share with you what I have learned.

Chapter 1

Identification, Diagnosis and Acceptance

Defining LD

Before any discussion on identifying learning disabilities (LD), a clear, acceptable definition of LD must be developed. For the purposes of this book, an abbreviated version of Public Law (PL) 94-142 is used. (See Chapter 3, "The Law Is On Your Side", Appendix C, "The Laws", and Appendix E, "IDEA Amendments of 1997".) In a nutshell, it states that children with special learning disabilities exhibit a disorder in one or more of the basic psychological processes involved in understanding or using spoken or written language.

LD *does not* include learning problems which are due primarily to visual, hearing or motor handicaps, mental retardation, or emotional disturbance. LD is a disorder of brain processing functions, *not* a psychological or behavioral problem

(Bernhard). LD, then, is a gap between ability and performance measured by either tests or course grades.

Identifying the Causes of LD

But just how or why does LD occur? Researchers, medical doctors, educators and other professionals differ on what causes LD. Some attribute heredity (see Chapter 6, "ADD and ADHD", for more information on genes), environmental factors such as drug and alcohol abuse, lead poisoning and pollution; others feel it is neurological. Of course, with the advances in medical technology, the survival rate for babies born prematurely has increased significantly. Unfortunately, as the preemie's life expectancy increases, so do the chances of LD and other lingering medical problems.

Although professionals do not agree on what is the cause of LD, they will agree and accept the following as true of children with LD (Bernhard):

—   The basic cause of school failure is NOT a lack of normal intelligence;
—   The basic cause is NOT a psychological problem;
—   The basic cause is NOT an obvious physical handicap; and
—   LD children do NOT learn the conventional way using standard teaching methods.

Suspecting LD

LD is sometimes referred to as the "invisible" disability because children with LD look and act intelligent and have no

The Most Common Characteristics of Children With Learning Disabilities

- Age-inappropriate hyperactivity, impulsivity, distractibility, inattention, short attention spans

- Difficulty with short- and long-term memory

- Disorganization

- Difficulty with academic skills in reading, writing, speech and mathematics

- Difficulty with fine (handwriting) and gross (running) motor skills

- Gaps in parts on IQ tests

- Lack of appropriate social and adaptive behavior (making and keeping friends)

- Speech, language and visual processing delays

- Transposing and/or confusing similar letters and order of letters

- Transposing and/or confusing similar numbers and sequences

- Low self-esteem

obvious physical handicaps. As a result, many times they are labeled "dumb", "lazy" and "stupid" in school, when, in fact, they are intelligent. They simply process information differently from those children without LD. Schools and families should always consider the possibility of an LD before assuming that a child who has been doing poorly in school is lazy or emotionally disturbed.

Several early clues indicate the presence of LD. In pre-school children, the failure to use language in communication by age three, or inadequate motor skills (buttoning, tying, climbing). In school-age children, a failure to learn skills that are appropriate to their grade is also an indicator.

The presence of one of the characteristics listed on the previous page does not mean your child is LD. However, if your child exhibits several of these characteristics, you should check with your family pediatrician. Ask your local school district what testing and screening programs are available for your child's age group. (See Chapter 5, "Testing, Record Keeping and Parent/Teacher Conferences", for more on testing.)

Diagnosing LD

When you realize that your child exhibits one or more of the listed characteristics, or you receive from your child's school a notice that your child will be tested or screened for *developmental delays* (a lag in mental or physical development), do not, and I emphasize DO NOT, feel alone. There are many professionals, schools and support groups which will guide you through the maze of living with a child with LD. Do not panic, but do talk to your family doctor and the local school system on testing for LD.

A *psychoeducational evaluation* is used to test your child

for LD, but do not let the evaluation name scare you. A psychoeducational evaluation is nothing more than a series of tests given to your child to determine if he or she has a learning disability.

If a disability is identified, these tests will help you understand the nature of it. The test results will show how the disability affects your child's learning, explain how your child processes information, describe the best way your child learns (learning style) and, finally, determine if your child qualifies for special education. (See Chapter 5, "Testing, Record Keeping and Parent/Teacher Conferences", for more on testing.)

Public school systems are required by PL 94-142 (see Chapter 3, "The Law Is On Your Side," for more complete information on the law) to provide psychoeducational evaluations for students in their district who are referred by their teacher(s) and other school personnel.

If the evaluation is done by your school district, it is usually done over a period of time which can take up to six months or longer, since it includes several professionals: the school counselor, school psychologist, school therapists, teachers, and other professionals.

If the school system does the evaluation, there is no fee. However, my strong recommendation is to have the school district do the first evaluation, but, as with any evaluation, get a second opinion.

Getting a Second Opinion

Depending on the locality, the private fee for the second opinion is at a minimum of $500, which your medical insurance may cover (check your policy).

Check with your family pediatrician for a recommended

psychologist to do your private testing, but make sure that the professional you select has experience in LD testing. Just as you would hire the right kind of doctor or attorney to meet your medical and legal needs, you need to hire a psychologist who specializes in LD problems and testing. Psychologists often specialize in one or two fields and, on occasion, will do LD testing.

Understanding Learning Styles

Since the psychoeducational evaluation usually takes several months to complete, the parents can begin a *learning styles inventory* on their child. Learning styles or modalities, as they are sometimes called, are nothing more than sensory channels used to acquire information.

Every person has his or her style of learning. Sometimes a variety of ways are used, but each person has his or her own particular style of learning. In a family with more than one child, parents can readily observe the various learning styles for each child. One child may be able to memorize a book read to him or her; another may need to see the written word and pictures to grasp the main ideas.

Individuals learn in three main ways: *auditory* (hearing), *visual* (seeing), and/or *kinesthetic* (touching). To better understand these three learning styles, imagine yourself at a party. How many times have you been introduced to a person only once and have been able to remember their name but not their face? If that describes you, then you are probably an auditory learner (one who learns by hearing). If you can remember the face but not the name, you are most likely a visual learner (one who learns by seeing). Kinesthetic learners (those who learn by touching) can remember the name and face only after they have written down the name. Many of us may use a combination of learning styles to achieve our goals, but whichever style(s) we employ as adults, we use the one that best fits our needs.

Although as adults we usually know what our particular learning style is and use it in our daily lives, young children, on the other hand, do not know their learning style — and that is where learning *styles* and learning *difficulties* clash.

Preschoolers and kindergarten/first graders use a learning process combining all three styles. This can be seen in such activities as listening, watching films and in drawing and writing. However, as the child advances in school, the learning process begins to focus much more on the auditory, and the rest is divided between visual and kinesthetic. At this level of school, the child who is an auditory learner excels, but, for the visual and kinesthetic learners, any underlying learning *problems* are significantly magnified (Tuttle and Paquette).

Keep in mind that *just because you or your child are a visual or kinesthetic learner, it does not mean you or your child are learning disabled.* For example, writing reminder lists for projects, tasks and errands does not mean you have a memory disability, it just means you need visual lists to remind you to get the tasks accomplished.

Learning styles play a very important part in a child's learning, so parents need to find the school and teacher who will teach to their child's learning style. Remember, the closer the match between a child's learning style and a teacher's teaching style, the more successful and rewarding the learning experience will be for both. This point will be stressed again when we get to the chapters on choosing the right school.

Educating Teachers About LD

Discovering your child's learning style and sharing that information with the teacher will help to ensure that classroom modifications and accommodations can take place. But remember, too, once LD, always LD, and knowing your child's learning style(s) is a giant step toward helping your child through school with a little less heartache and a lot more success.

Current efforts to provide instructional services for students with LD are hindered because most classroom teachers are unaware of the specific disabilities at the root of the student's academic problems. Public school teachers in particular, because of sheer numbers of students assigned for each class, teach to the masses and are not required to take LD training. They are sometimes being asked to work in the dark when it comes to teaching a child with LD. Fortunately, some state legislatures are getting involved and are requiring a recommended number of LD courses for teacher certification.

Without a good understanding of basic LD problems and their compensating strengths, the classroom teacher does not have the information necessary to make appropriate modifications for a particular student. Only when the parents and the school are in agreement, and understand the full meaning of the disability, can a meaningful academic education plan be worked out for your child's best interest.

Learn to be your child's advocate and to teach your child to advocate for him or herself at an appropriate age. Advocacy requires direct involvement and active negotiating on your child's behalf. It also necessitates the ongoing supervision of your child's program, services, healthcare and school.

In other words, you need to become the intermediary between your child and the outside world. Do not rely solely on the school system and professionals to tell you how to educate your child. Learn everything you can about your child's disability so that you can educate the school system if needed.

You may find that some teachers, during your child's educational career, will be quite knowledgeable about LD and will customize the way they teach your child. However, other teachers may not be so accommodating, which will require you to play a more active role. (This may even include "doing battle" with the teacher(s) and the school system.)

Keeping Your Cool

During this time of testing and screening, it is only natural for your emotions to be running high. When you finally receive the test results confirming or denying that your child is LD, the emotional toll can be almost more than you can handle, and its stress on the entire family can be devastating (See Chapter 4, "The Role of the Family"). To help center yourself, and your family, remind yourself of the following:

—   The worst thing you can do is blame yourself.
—   You are not alone in this. According to the National Center for Learning Disabilities (NCLD), between 10 and 15 percent of the U.S. population (parents and children alike) has some form of LD.
—   Parent support groups can be helpful. Local chapters of CHADD, LDA and sibling support programs such as Sibshops, an award-winning program that brings together 8-13 year old brothers and sisters of children with special needs and Sibling Support Project (SSP), a national program dedicated to the interests of brothers and sisters of people with special health and developmental needs, can

all provide tremendous relief and an outlet to validate your emotions as well as help siblings. (See Chapter 4, "The Role of the Family," for information and listing of nationally recognized support groups)

—   It is essential to recognize LD and related problems as early as possible.

—   Without recognition and help (from you and the educational system), your child will become increasingly frustrated and distressed as he or she persistently fails. By the time your child reaches high school, he or she may give up!

—   When you recognize early and treat appropriately, your child can learn to compensate for his or her disabilities.

—   All children have strengths and weaknesses — so your child really is not that different from the next child — he or she simply processes information in a different way.

Focus your energies on how to teach to your child's strengths and properly adjust to dealing with the disability. As parents, we look at our children as a reflection of ourselves, and when there is the slightest hint of a disability — whether it is a physical or mental disability — we all too often assign blame to ourselves. So, above all else, *do not blame yourself!* Take the time necessary to accept and understand that your child is LD. Once you do, you will move forward.

Several years ago, I attended an LD workshop during which the speaker read the piece on the following page, which to this day I have kept and used when my emotions get the best of me. As the essay so eloquently points out, learning that your child is LD is sometimes hard to accept. Grieving is part of the acceptance process, so take this time with confidence and remember it is not YOUR fault.

WELCOME TO HOLLAND
by Emily Pearl Kingsley
(Reprinted by permission
from *LDA Newsbrief*, May-June, 1991)

I am often asked to describe the experience of raising a child with a disability to try to help people who have not shared that unique experience to understand it, to imagine how it would feel. It's like this:

When you are going to have a baby, it's like planning a fabulous vacation trip – to Italy. You buy a bunch of guidebooks and make your wonderful plans. The coliseum, Michelangelo's David, the gondolas in Venice. You may learn some handy phrases in Italian. Its all very exciting.

After months of eager anticipation, the day finally arrives. You pack your bags and off you go. Several hours later, the plane lands. The stewardess comes in and says, "Welcome to Holland."

"Holland?!?" you say. "What do you mean, Holland? I signed up for Italy! I'm supposed to be in Italy. All my life I've dreamed of going to Italy." But there's been a change in the flight plan. They've landed in Holland and there you must stay.

The important thing is that they haven't taken you to a horrible, disgusting, filthy place, full of pestilence, famine and disease. It's just a different place. So you must go out and buy new guidebooks. And you must learn a whole new language. And you will meet a whole new group of people you would have never met.

It's just a different place. It's slower-paced than Italy, less flashy than Italy. But after you've been there for a while and you catch your breath, you look around, and you begin to notice that Holland has windmills, Holland has tulips, Holland even has Rembrandts.

But everyone you know is busy coming and going from Italy, and they're all bragging about what a wonderful time they had there. And for the rest of your life, you will say, "Yes, that's where I was supposed to go. That's what I had planned."

The pain of that will never, ever, ever go away, because the loss of that dream is a very significant loss. But if you spend your life mourning the fact that you didn't get to Italy, you may never be free to enjoy the very special, the very lovely things about Holland.

In a Nutshell . . .

— LD is basically a gap between one's ability and performance.
— LD is a problem of brain processing, not a psychological or behavior problem.
— Get a second opinion on the diagnosis.
— Learn and understand your child's learning style. The closer the match between a child's learning style and the teacher's teaching approach, the more successful your child will be in his or her learning.
— It takes time to accept that your child is LD.
— Do not blame yourself.

Frequently Asked Questions Concerning Learning Disabilities

What is a learning disability?

In general, a learning disability is a problem in acquiring and using skills required for listening, speaking, reading, writing, reasoning and mathematical ability. Such problems in the acquisition of skills cannot be traced to inadequate intelligence, school environment, emotional problems, visual or hearing defects, cultural deprivation, or lack of motivation.

What kinds of symptoms signal a possible learning disability?

There is a variety of symptoms that may signal the presence of such a problem. Some of the more common include disorganization, poor muscle coordination, impulsivity, distractibility, short attention span, trouble in completing assignments, poor spelling, poor handwriting, poor social skills, low reading level, difficulty in following directions, transposing numbers and sequences and letters and order of letters, discrepancy between ability and performance, and language difficulties.

Are dyslexia and learning disabilities the same?

No. Dyslexia is a *specific form* of LD, many times severe. Dyslexia refers to a problem in learning how to read. Children with LD are not dyslexic; however, all dyslexic children are LD.

Are reversals an indication of a learning disability?

Reversals of letters and numbers are common in children up to grade 3 and may not by themselves indicate any LD. However, if a child frequently reverses letters and numbers along with other symptoms or continues after age 8, parents should discuss this with a professional or the child's teacher as soon as possible.

Can a child be LD in only one area?

Yes. Some children may have a learning disability in only one area, such as short-term memory, mathematical computations, spelling, or reading comprehension. Of course, the more areas affected, the more serious the disability.

Can a true learning disability show up in later grades with no earlier indications?

In most cases, a true learning disability has a historical pattern. With advances in medical science, especially with regard to premature babies, learning disabilities are apparent well before schooling begins.

What is the first thing to do if I suspect that my child may have a learning disability?

Contact your school psychologist and your child's teacher and make them aware of your concerns. Ask for a psychoeducational evaluation. The school should have identified this possibility before you did. If you do not wish to go through the school, you can contact a qualified professional in the field, or a clinic that specializes in learning disabilities. They will be happy to evaluate your child. Keep in mind, however, that a private evaluation can be very expensive, while it is free through the public school system.

Must my child be placed in special education if he or she has a learning disability?

Not necessarily. It is the legal and moral responsibility of every school district to refer such a child for a review before the CSE (Committee on Special Education). A review does not mean immediate classification. It just means that enough evidence exists to warrant a "look" by the district. If the child has a learning disability and is encountering frustration in school, then the services he or she will receive should greatly reduce such problems. Also, remember that as parents you must agree to the special education placement of your child, the school district cannot just assign your child to a special education class without your permission.

See also "Suggested Reading" for Chapter 1, pp. 269-70.

Chapter 2

Self-Esteem and Social Development

Understanding Your Child's Self-Esteem

Many factors are very important in understanding the emotional makeup of a child with LD. The child's developmental history, the family's treatment of him or her, the child's peers' reaction to him or her, his or her success and/or frustration in school, and the learning disability itself are all elements crucial to understanding why a child behaves and feels as he or she does. However, the common denominator in all children with LD, regardless of the reason, is a decrease in his or her self-esteem.

This chapter is placed near the beginning of the book because the three most important aspects in the emotional life of a child with LD are self-esteem, self-esteem and self-esteem. The term *self-esteem* is certainly one of the most overused buzz words in education and psychology. It seems that almost every failure – educational or personal – is blamed on "low self-esteem." Unfortunately, this overuse has caused many of us to downplay the importance of our feelings about ourselves.

A child receives the first input when the mother holds him or her as a baby in the hospital. That process continues on a daily basis as the child interacts with parents, relatives, teachers and peers. What those people say *to* your child, *about* your child, and the body language they use in their encounters *with* your child, provide him or her with the basis for the feelings your child has about himself or herself.

Because a child with LD encounters more negative situations (beyond their control) than other children, he or she will probably encounter more derogatory remarks than will other children. Adults who do not fully understand the nature of LD (as well as those who should know better) often perceive these children as uncooperative, lazy and incapable, and they often have no qualms about telling the children about their failings.

Children do not readily forget such painful encounters. They incorporate criticisms into their own self-concept. Little by little, they begin to believe they are dumb, stupid, lazy, difficult to be around, a burden to their family, or an embarrassment. Some even begin to label themselves as a "retard". These negative effects may not manifest themselves until months or years later, and they can culminate in depression, anger, misbehavior, self-doubt, manipulative behavior, stress, irresponsibility and general emotional disharmony.

It is always difficult to explain to any struggling child why some things in life are not easy to accomplish or achieve. It is even harder to explain to the child with LD why life is at times so much more of a task for him or her than it is for his or her siblings or friends. Unfortunately for the child with LD, life becomes a vicious cycle: first, the child is angry about his life; this anger fuels more self-doubt; this self-doubt causes more failure, which creates more anger and more self-doubt.

Considerable evidence exists in professional journals to illustrate the important relationship between our *feelings* about how we will perform and how we actually do perform. Many students who encounter problems in school do not feel they are capable of success. Therefore, they do not try.

Priscilla Vail, in her book *Smart Kids with School Problems* (New American Library), has identified six emotional difficulties that can accompany a learning disability:

— Fear of failure
— Disorganization (the inability to make sense of the world because of lack of *affect*)
— Fear of depletion (unwillingness to offer what little skills or energy is available)
— Learned helplessness (lack of a sense of control over life because effort brings no results)
— Guilt
— Depression

Not *every* child with LD has *all* these emotions, and they may appear in varying degrees. However, problems like these lead to low self-esteem and little, if any, self-confidence. A result of this low self-esteem is a sense of being a failure as a person. This does not stop with childhood but can and will follow a person throughout life. Without help, the anger, frustration, aggressiveness, withdrawal and noncompliance will be the norm in relationships of all kinds. The problems can involve family, friends, spouses and co-workers.

Understanding Your Child's Anger

The anger of children with LD occurs at home, at school, and with peers. First, the child is angry at the parents. Children, in general, like to blame their parents when something goes wrong, and children with LD, in particular, blame the parents for their LD. They know that the LD is not really caused by their parents, but they are angry because their parents have such high expectations of them. When the child wants sympathy because he or she has LD, the parents expect performance and make him or her do his or her homework, do chores and participate as a family member. The child with LD also knows he or she cannot survive without parents, and this dependency fuels more anger.

Anger and dependency are hard emotions for any child to handle, but they are especially hard for the child with LD, who has a tougher time sorting out information and emotions. Because the child with LD is volatile, distractible, and easily provoked, he or she is an easy prey for sibling rivalry (see Chapter 4, "The Role of the Family").

Siblings of the child with LD create yet another vicious cycle. Children with LD fight with their siblings, ruin their toys and projects, and worst yet, embarrass them in front of their friends. Retaliation is the sibling's only option. The result: sibling rivalry. The child with LD demands more time from the parents, who feel sorry for their child with LD, and this makes the siblings even more jealous. In the end, the siblings as well as the child with LD are angry. It is a no-win situation for the parents.

However, the stress and tensions that home life can produce are nothing compared to the painful realities of the LD child's attempts to make social contact with his or her peers. At home, no matter how bad it gets, there is security, forgiveness and love. Outside the family there is no safety net. The child with LD desperately wants to belong but, often, fitting in or having friends is difficult. As a result, the child may be subjected to teasing, or, even worse, to ostracism. Children are notoriously cruel to one another, and, regardless of the school's or the parents' attempts to socially mainstream the child with LD, the child is often perceived as different – a terrible stigma in childhood.

Improving Your Child's Self-Esteem

The good news is that the self-esteem of children with LD can be improved. The following suggestions can be incorporated in your family's daily activities, and if these suggestions work at home, suggest that these ideas be incorporated in your child's educational plan, as well.

Provide opportunities which will build on your child's strengths and interests. Find and develop their special talents, both in and out of school. If swimming is their best sport, pursue it – even at the cost of less time for study. Remember, self-esteem develops through a sense of accomplishment in *life*, not necessarily in *school*. Help your child find those special talents and teach your child to use them to his or her advantage.

Discuss with your child his or her disability. Do so in an appropriate level of language and as clearly as possible. By showing that you understand the problems and feelings that your child experiences on a daily basis, the child then knows he or she is not alone and can start feeling understood. He or she will also know that you provide a basis for support and communication, that you are on their side.

Praise demonstrated *effort* rather than *results*. We seem to measure everything in results, but for the child with LD, effort should be just as important, especially if the effort comes in an area of his or her weakness. Give compliments honestly, freely, and in large doses. Remember how you feel when someone notices something positive about you. Remember, a little praise goes a long way.

Give your child choices. Choices do not have to be sophisticated or monumental but can be as simple as, "Would you like spaghetti or lasagna for dinner?" or "Do you want to see this movie or that one?" By giving choices, you help your child become more self-reliant through developing problem-solving and decision-making skills.

Offer assistance and not demands. Help the child get started on a project such as homework, cleaning their room or raking the yard. A team approach will make a large task seem much smaller and not so overwhelming. Just a little help, especially in getting organized, will help the child see an end to the project.

Involve your child in noncompetitive sports or creative activities. Children with LD need recreational activities even more than additional hours of homework. Finding noncompetitive participation in activities such as horseback riding, swimming, computer games, drawing, singing and dancing will give the child with LD a sense of competence and assurance with friends and classmates.

Allow your child the opportunity to repeat successful

experiences. A foundation of positive experiences is necessary for self-esteem. Any opportunity to repeat success can only be an ego-inflating experience. For example, if your child excels in swimming and enjoys the activity, why not allow your child a few extra minutes or laps and encourage your child to enter swim meets? Whether your child is LD or not, one-on-one competition can be good for the self-esteem, especially if your child wins. But do not force the competition issue.

Use the reward system to shape positive behavior. Punishment tells a child what not to do while reward informs a child what is acceptable behavior. Rewarding positive behavior increases self-esteem. We usually think of rewards as monetary, but they need not be. Rewards can be in the form of special trips and dinners or as simple as extra television time.

Help your child set realistic goals. Set several smaller goals rather one huge or final goal. At the same time, help your child find a way to accomplish the goals. Remember, success breeds success.

Not all the above suggestions will work, but those of us who live and work with children with LD have innumerable opportunities to enhance their self-esteem by being sensitive to their needs and challenges. Neither parents nor educators can afford to ignore a child's self-esteem in their zeal to help them overcome their problems in learning.

Understanding Your Child's Social Development

Becoming a socialized human being is a complex process. It is especially hard for children who are LD. Compen-

sating for an academic deficiency is easy compared to perceiving, understanding and reacting to life's events. Children
who are struggling in the classroom often experience difficulties in their out-of-school lives, too.

From early childhood throughout our entire lives, we join
others in play and work. These people form our peer groups.
For children with LD, interacting with peers may be the *most*
difficult task, because their problems with communications
and interactions often lead to rejection by their peers.

Communication takes two forms: spoken and non-spo-
ken. Both are difficult for the child with LD. They tend to say
whatever comes to mind and, as a result, embarrass and be-
wilder their families and potential friends, as well as themselves. They cannot keep secrets for family or peers, and they
never seem to know when to speak and when to be quiet.

This inability to communicate may reflect to a large extent the same neurological immaturity that forms the basis for
the LD problem. For example, children with a faulty judgment
of space, who trip because they do not notice what is close
and what is far away, have trouble looking at others and relating
to them. Children who cannot distinguish between *the same as,
different from* and *equal to* may fail in socialization because they
are unable to correctly evaluate a social situation and determine
what communication or behavior is appropriate. Children may
say the right thing but say it to the wrong person; they may sit
quietly, not interacting, in a festive situation; or they may cling to
one person and keep up a constant barrage of conversation directed only at that one person. These social failures can be due
to problems in more general cognitive areas – problems in such
areas as estimating, differentiating, making inferences and
understanding proportion (Smith 170).

Nonverbal communication is just as difficult. Reading the
facial expressions and gestures which comprise body language

is more difficult than reading words. Listening is often already a problem with these children, and many cannot distinguish between different tones or inflections of others' voices. Body language and social cues are frequently far too abstract for the child with LD to comprehend.

Interactions with peers pose serious problems. Playing even simple board games creates difficulties because some last too long, and children with LD lose their focus. Sports can also create problems. Sometimes lack of coordination and lack of spatial perception lead to failure at sports. Children with LD can suffer from the "me" syndrome and usually demand that *they* be the center of every game, every sport and every event. The immaturity of these children also creates major problems with socialization in sports.

Improving Your Child's Weaknesses

Parents of children with LD have many obstacles to face in rearing their child. It is hard enough to teach them how to compensate for an academic deficiency, but it is even harder to teach socialization. Help is available either through the school system or privately and, of course, parents, grandparents, aunts and uncles can help, too.

Social skills needed for social competence include physical factors such as eye contact and posture, social responsibilities such as sharing, and interaction skills such as initiating and maintaining conversations. If your child does not pick up social cues or has poor social skills, he or she might benefit from a form of group therapy called *social skills training*. Sometimes this is done as part of the special education program by the school psychologist or counselor. Social skills training focuses on developing an awareness of and sensitivity to his or her social problems and finding alternative solutions for the identified problems. Finally, the child links the new knowledge to past events as well as to future happenings.

Another type of therapy used in teaching social skills is *language therapy.* Relating to others depends upon clear communication of needs, feelings, understanding and appreciation. Children with LD may need years before they can begin to talk easily and to say exactly what they mean. Others never reach a point at which communication becomes easy, fluent and unrestrained. Language therapy can help.

Language therapy provides help in actually *organizing* language. A language pathologist or therapist works on syntax and language structure, and on how to summarize and speak succinctly, and how to ask questions. Practice in daily communication skills such as greetings and brief chitchat, and practice in the art of conversation are also the realm of the language therapist.

Play therapy can be used for the child who cannot say how he or she feels. It is especially useful for emotional and behavioral problems as well as social problems due to depression, death of a loved one, divorce and abuse. Children are, by nature, playful. Given a few props and some time, play is the natural behavior of young children. It is also the most powerful way that children learn. For example, when pretending, children can master frightening feelings through play and practice the social skills needed when they are older. For the child with LD, all of this can be beneficial.

Both a school psychologist and a language therapist should be available through the school system. If your child is in the special education program at the school, try to get this service written into the educational plan (see Chapter 3, "The Law Is On Your Side" for more on educational plans). If your child is not part of the special education program, these services may be available at your child's school or through the school district. Your child might be able to participate without charge. Chances are good that the services are available – if you ask.

In addition to therapy sessions, there are several things that parents and the school system can work on to help. To foster social development, parents can:

— Provide good role models themselves
— Explain what is appropriate behavior so that a child understands what is expected
— Praise positive social behavior at the time it occurs
— Foster a sense of belonging by including and making sure your son or daughter participates in family outings and activities
— Discuss interpersonal conflicts when they arise and suggest alternative ways of handling them
— Encourage communication with your child so that their problems and concerns can be shared
— Encourage social independence and self-reliance

If your child is to become socially competent, teachers need to be part of the solution. Schools provide opportunities for social as well as academic learning. Social skills can be taught as an integral part of a school program. A comprehensive social curriculum includes the teaching of both social perception and social behavior. At every level, the school needs to promote communication skills, sensitivity to others, self-awareness and self-control. Make sure the school that your child attends offers or fosters this type of social behavior. In addition to achieving the above goals, teachers can

— Use the buddy system or peer pairing when appropriate

How to Communicate With Your Children

Communication is a two-way street. Talking and listening are both part of communication. Use the "I'll talk and you listen, and then you talk and I'll listen" technique as a first step in developing communication with your child.

Don't "attack" when communicating your feelings. When communicating feelings, try using the words "I," "we" or "me" as often as possible and avoid the word "you." Try to focus on your feelings rather than on the other's behavior. Tell your child how the behavior affected you.

Teach children to label feelings properly. Children may have a difficult time communicating because they lack the experience in labeling their feelings. It is, therefore, crucial for parents to assist their children in correctly labeling a feeling or emotion. Show them, explain the difference between anger, frustration, jealousy, etc.

Remember that all behavior has a trigger. If parents can trace back children's responses to the source or trigger, they will have a very good chance of identifying the real problem. Remember that all behavior is a message, and for many children their behavior is the only means of communicating their frustrations or feelings. The problem is that such behavior is frequently misunderstood and misinterpreted – resulting in more problems.

Beware of nonverbal misinterpretations. For the child with LD, body language is about as foreign as it gets. Yet in our everyday lives we need to know and understand body language. Let your child know when you are upset, angry or frustrated so that they may learn from you about feelings and emotions via body language.

Use written communication whenever possible. Children with LD may have problems with writing, but parents do not have an excuse; therefore, notes thanking a child for some positive behavior or telling him or her how proud you are of her or him are just two examples that parents can use.

Try to use direct love as often as possible. A primary need for any individual at any age is the need to feel loved and cared for. Examples of direct love include hugging, kissing, cuddling, holding and stroking.

–   Provide discussion time for airing problems in class
–   Keep competitiveness to a minimum
–   Reward positive behavior
–   Incorporate weekly social skills in lesson plans

Social problems that are ignored at a younger age can and usually do persist into adulthood. To see a child socially isolated or rejected hurts parents, teachers and caring adults. The pain, embarrassment and suffering caused by a child's unhappiness pervades everyone around the child. Seek competent professionals to assist you to help your child achieve the social competence that will have lifelong effects on your child's happiness and success in life.

In a Nutshell . . .

–   The most important aspect of a child's emotional life is self-esteem.
–   Low self-esteem fosters anger, frustration, aggressiveness, and withdrawal in relationships of all kinds.
–   Social skills therapy, language therapy, and play therapy can be used to teach social skills.
–   Social problems can last a lifetime if ignored early.

Frequently Asked Questions
Concerning Self-Esteem and Social Development

Why did my youngest child develop low self-esteem while my oldest child has always had a very high self-esteem?

Why one child has more self-esteem than another is hard to explain, but parents, relatives, siblings, teachers, professionals and peers all play a role. What these people say to your child, about your child, and the body language they use in their encounters with your child provide him or her with the basis for the feelings your child has about himself or herself.

Is there anything a parent can do to help a child increase self-esteem?

There are several things that you can do at home (listed in this chapter) which can help raise your child's self-esteem, but the important point here is that if it works at home, try to get your child's teacher(s) to also use the same techniques at school.

My son attends a public school. Do you know which programs are usually available through the public school system to help my child with socialization?

As brought out in Chapter 7, "School Option #1: Public Schools", not all school systems, school districts nor even state DOEs are created equal. However, most schools will have available a school psychologist and a language therapist to help your child with socialization. It is quite possible that your school or district also has a play therapist available. If your child is in the special education program, this type of help can be written into the IEP (see Chapter 3, "The Law Is On Your Side", for more information on IEP). Otherwise, find out from your school office which professionals are available either at your son's school or through the district office. Then set up appointments with each and explain why you think your child should be treated. Chances are, they will help your child through therapy that is offered at your child's school. If the services you request are not available, ask for recommendations of a qualified therapist. Many times, school professionals will also have a private practice on the side. However, do not feel obligated to use the school professional. In fact, you should interview several therapists, then select one who would work best with your child.

Will public school teach social skills to my child with LD?

Yes, through social skills training. Social skills training can also be put into the IEP – just be sure to request it if your child is eligible.

My son is signed up for language therapy to help him with social skills training. How will that help him?

With the help of a language therapist or pathologist, a child can learn how to better communicate as well as express feelings. Practice in daily communication skills, such as greetings and brief chitchat, and practice in the art of conversation are also part of language therapy, which ultimately helps in social skills therapy.

See also "Suggested Reading" for Chapter 2, pp. 270-71.

Chapter 3

The Law Is On Your Side

Believe it or not, parents, after years of paying income taxes and watching Congress pass one law after another, *there are at least two laws which are on your side!* This chapter will help you understand these laws, and, at the same time, it will give enough information so you will know your legal rights. Understanding the laws will help you become a true advocate for your child. The two laws which will be examined in this chapter are: the Individuals with Disabilities Education Act (IDEA), passed in 1990, and Section 504 of the Rehabilitation Act of 1973.

Understanding IDEA

Individuals with Disabilities Education Act (IDEA) — Before diving into "guts" of the law, a brief history is needed. In 1975,

PL (Public Law) 94-142, The *Education of All Handicapped Children Act* mandated that all school-age children with disabilities receive a free appropriate education in the least restrictive environment (LRE). The law further stipulates that schools provide the children with needed special education and related services. Related services include such services as transportation, physical therapy (PT), occupational therapy (OT), adapted physical education and psychological assessments.

In 1986, the amendment to this bill, the *Individuals with Disabilities Education Act Amendments*, extended the mandate to provide all of the services to the 3- to 5-year-old population (Part B), and offered additional incentives to provide early intervention programs for infants and toddlers with disabilities (from birth through 2-year-old population), found in Part H of the law. In 1990, this law was amended again, and among other things, it changed the name of the legislation to the *Individuals with Disabilities Education Act* or IDEA. This was amended only once in 1993. The IDEA legislation is a very important federal law to understand because it requires that a free appropriate public education, which includes special education and related services, be available to children and youth with disabilities in mandated age ranges. You can get your copy of the entire law by contacting your Congressman or Congresswoman. Also, it is quite possible that you can obtain a copy from the Internet (see Appendix E, "IDEA Amendments of 1997"), as there is a movement in Washington to have laws available to the public through the computer. Check with your local Congressperson or call LDA at (412) 341-1515.

The main points of IDEA are as follows:

—   ALL children with disabilities must be provided with a free and appropriate education.

— children between ages 3 and 21 will be educated at no cost to you, even if your local school district does not have a program that is right for your child with disabilities.

— If your community does not or cannot educate your child within the school system, the school system will have to pay for a program in another city, town or private placement — whichever is most appropriate.

The law also defines "children with disabilities" to include those

"with mental retardation, hearing impairments including deafness, speech or language impairments, visual impairments including blindness, serious emotional disturbance, orthopedic impairments, autism, traumatic brain injury, other health impairments or specific learning disabilities and who, by reason thereof need special education and related services."

The following process must take place if you or a school staff member suspects your child needs special education:

— *A referral is made* by you or your child's teacher to the special education department of your child's school.

— *A pre-assessment conference is held* between the parent (guardian) and the special education coordinator of your child's school before the assessment takes place. At that time, you will be given information on the psychoeducational evaluation (see Chapter 1, "Identification, Diagnosis and Acceptance") that is used to test children with disabilities. The parent (guardian) must consent in writing before the evaluation can begin.

— *Your child will be evaluated* by a team of professionals

Individual Educational Plan (IEP)

The IEP is the "heart and soul" of IDEA. The IEP is the written education plan that your child will follow during that school year and consists of

- A profile of your child's strengths and weaknesses and medical and educational history

- Current performance levels in all areas for which your child will be receiving help

- Annual goals for progress based on your child's current performance level and short-term instructional objectives to achieve the annual goals

- The methods and materials to be used to help meet those goals

- The amount of time your child will receive special education services as well as regular education classes in which your child will participate, if any

- The dates for the beginning and ending point of the services

- The method the school district will use to determine whether the short-term instructional objectives are being achieved

Sample IEP Form
Individualized Educational Plan

Student Data

Student Name:_____Date of Birth:_____
Parent(s) Names:_____
Address:_____
Home Telephone:_____
Dominant Language-Home:_____ Dominant Language-Student:_____

Recommendations

Classification:_____ Grade:_____
Placement:_____
Class Size/Ratio:_____ Length of Program:_____
Program Initiation Date:_____ Diploma:_____
Transportation Required:_____
Annual Review Date:_____ Triennial Date:_____

IQ Test Information

Verbal IQ_____ Performance IQ_____Full Scale IQ_____
Foreign Language Exempt: yes_____ no_____
Physical Education Recommendation: Regular_____ Adaptive_____
Related Services Recommended: (Check off those recommended and fill in suggested information)

Service

Sessions   WK Minutes/Session
____Resource Room   _____/_____
____Speech/Language   _____/_____
____Physical Therapy   _____/_____
____Occupational Therapy   _____/_____
____Art Therapy   _____/_____
____In-School Counseling
    Individual or Group (Circle)_____/_____

Computer Sources for the Child with LD

The use of computers and other assistive devices for children, youth and adults with LD has been growing in popularity and is reflected in the development of resources that students, parents, teachers and even employers can use to check out appropriate technology. Following is a list of national organizations which provide information about computers and other machines and their adaptability for specific disabilities. They will also answer questions about suitable software programs.

I might also mention that, if you can have available information on the technology your child could use in and out of the classroom *prior* to the IEP meeting, it might be possible to have that information written into the IEP. And if your child is part of inclusion (see Chapter 7, "Public Schools"), share with the teacher(s) the technology information that your child will use or will need to use to succeed in their classroom. In other words, come prepared for either meeting.

The Center for Special Education Technology, funded by the U.S. Department of Education, is jointly sponsored by Council for Exceptional Children, JWK International and LINC Resources. The center's toll-free number is 1-800-345-TECH (in Virginia it is 703-750-0500). Hours are 1:00-6:00 pm, EST.

SRI reviews software programs for handicapped children and youth. Its toll-free number is 1-800-327-5892, and it is open from 9:00 am to 5:00 pm, EST.

Closing the Gap evaluates software and hardware for handicapped users. It also publishes a newsletter. For information, write to Closing the Gap, P.O. Box 68, Henderson, MN 56044.

ABLEDATA has a computerized listing for commercially available products for all types of disabilities. The address is ABLEDATA, National Rehabilitation Information Center, The Catholic University of America, 4407 - 8th St., NE, Washington, DC 20017, phone (202) 635-5822.

who will look for specific strengths and weaknesses to determine if there is a need for special education services. Your child will be assessed in the area of the suspected disability; however, you can ask that other areas also be assessed. The tests administered cannot be racially biased and must be in your child's native language. The evaluation process is a *team* process; therefore, no single opinion or evaluation will be used. As the parent of the child with the disability, you are also member of the team.

— *Within 45 school days, the school must evaluate your child, conduct a team meeting, and develop an appropriate educational plan.* The first 30 days are for the evaluation, and the next 15 days are for the meeting and writing the Individual Educational Plan (IEP). All professionals who conducted assessments of your child should be at this meeting. Each report should include specific strengths and weaknesses and recommendation for remediation. If a special need is indicated, an IEP will be written, detailing the placement recommended and the services to be provided.

At this point, I would like to comment on annual goals and accommodations as related to the IEP. While it has become increasingly acceptable to add goals and objectives pertaining to the acquisition of computer skills, it is *rare* that the computer has been included in a student's IEP as an *actual* accommodation. This is understandable, because computers are expensive. The daily use of a computer can be of immense help to a child with LD. Whether the child is 4 or 14, the computer can help with reading, letter formation and writing.

The current status of this viable solution for the child with LD is more dependent upon economics than educational validation. If a computer would help your child with language or fine motor skills, try to have your team write computer usage into the IEP. If computer time and usage is added in and your school does not have a computer lab or the classroom does not have a computer for your child to use, then the school district will have to come up with the funds to accommodate your child's use of the computer.

Understanding Accommodations

The 504 Accommodation Plan is a plan developed by the school professionals, which can include the teacher(s), counselor, psychologist and any other professionals who may be assigned to work with your child. Parents are also encouraged to be involved. Together, the team will develop a plan that will help your child work, function and learn more easily in a regular classroom. The plan should cover the physical arrangement of the room (for example: seating your child near the teacher), lesson presentation (for example: providing a peer notetaker or the use of a tape recorder), assignments/ worksheets (for example: giving extra time to complete tasks), test taking (for example: untimed tests, open-book tests), organization (for example: sending weekly/daily progress reports home), behavior (for example: giving extra privileges and rewards, allowing short breaks between assignments), and any other accommodations that the professionals feel may help your child learn. Basically, as the name states, the plan accommodates learning. For the child who has difficulty learning but does not qualify under IDEA, the Accommodation Plan is the next best tool to help in the learning process. Classroom accommodations (tools and services which can help your child overcome a disability) can also include the following:

- Taped textbooks, available through Recording for the Blind
- Extended time for taking tests
- Tutoring
- Use of a notetaker – for students who have trouble both listening in class *and* taking notes
- Use of a scribe (one who copies writing), during test taking – for students who have trouble writing but who can express their answers verbally to the scribe, who writes down the responses
- Use of a reader during test taking– for students who have trouble reading test questions
- Tape recording of class lectures
- Testing in a quiet place – for students who are easily distracted (ADD/ADHD students, for example)

Participating in IEP Team Meetings

Each child served under this law must have an IEP developed at a meeting of the special education team that evaluated your child. *You are a member of that team.* You must be notified in advance of the meeting so that you and all team members can be in attendance.

As a parent member of the IEP team, it is imperative that you understand the terminology used by the professionals when developing the IEP. If you do not understand and/or do not agree, you need to speak up *then* and not be afraid to speak up *often*. Remember, you have the right to accept or reject any or all of the services indicated or to request an independent evaluation. At the end of this chapter are a few helpful hints to make the IEP meeting a meaningful and productive experience.

Ten Ways to Take Charge of Your Child's IEP Meeting or Family Support Plan

By Janet Holmes
(Reprinted by permission from *Family News Digest*)

Be first . . . make sure you talk first. Don't be afraid to lead the IEP meeting. Bring notes, take notes and make all introductions yourself. It's your school, your teachers, your child. Put your priorities on the table for discussion first.

Plan ahead . . . choose your guests purposefully. Make sure the right people attend and plan to stay. If you have specific or big concerns, make sure decision makers are there to answer the appropriate questions. Know the amount of time you need and don't take time off work to attend a meeting that has the most important people leaving first or not there at all. Don't be afraid to include other related community service providers. As a courtesy, make sure the teacher is aware of who will attend.

Build a Strong Base of Information. You know your child. Get to know his school behavior, attend his class for a substantial amount of time. Be sure to use the appropriate visiting procedures but don't be afraid to make a surprise visit. Make sure your expectations are realistic and be willing to visit new programs. During the IEP meeting ask questions if you do not understand. You are the expert for your child, but you are not expected to understand all school terminology.

Know Your Rights . . . Public Law has given all parents rights and schools legal responsibilities. How can you advocate for important issues if you're not sure you are right? Local family and state organizations hold workshops for parents. Find them!

Bring Notes . . . make your own goals for your child. Start with making long-term goals for your child and family. Involve family members by asking for their input. Review your old plan, study the form and how the professionals write the "goals." Take your own notes to the meeting and write long- and short-term objectives in your words. It is appropriate to include your suggestions, you should expect nothing less. If there is nothing on the old plan that means anything to you or your child and family, do your own homework.

continued on the next page

continued from the facing page

Know How to Say No . . . be gracefully firm. Take a firm stand on important issues and only important ones. Be willing to compromise and don't expect to get it all. Choose your fight carefully, and then use the phrase "that is unacceptable." Have your argument ready, but always speak carefully. Get areas of disagreement written on the plan or, better yet, go home and write a letter to attach to the IEP. Have your support person ready to help, which may give you time to think. Don't be rushed into accepting anything; IEP's can be continued at a later date. The IEP will go forward without your signature, but you need to document your disagreement in case you wish to take the issue to due process.

Make Friends . . . at school. Always support your school and teacher. Be the room mother, volunteer to help whenever you can. If you are respected as a supporter of the school, you are more likely to be respected at the IEP. Let people know you appreciate them, make positive comments. A few kind words can only open doors for you and your child.

Keep Your Cool . . . angry parents are sometimes written off. Take your spouse or a friend to the IEP meeting. Although anger is sometimes needed to get your point across, remember, parents who lose their temper are quickly labeled as uncooperative and unreasonable which can make it easier for personnel to gather others against your ideas and concerns. No matter how right you are, your anger could be used against you in all future dealings with the school. Again, always try to be gracefully firm.

Keep Records . . . put it on paper. Maintain records for your child. Put all your correspondence in the file. Make every IEP request in writing and ask for a written response. If you call, note the time requesting a meeting or requesting anything how can you prove later that a request was made. Phone calls can be exaggerated and go from a simple request to a major confrontation. You have a legal right to review your child's school records. Check every so often to see if your correspondences are included.

End Your IEP . . . with a good check up. At the end of the IEP, make sure all of your points have been included. Check up on the promises, goals, and objectives that were agreed upon at the meeting. It is *your* job to monitor the IEP plan. It is appropriate to update, add to, or change an IEP goal. This must be done by convening another IEP meeting. Make the request in writing. Maybe only a few people may need to attend.

The criteria used for determining whether a child is LD are quite specific. Your child's team determines whether your child has a specific learning disability based on several tests and evaluations. Remember, no *single* item can be the determining factor as to whether or not your child has a specific learning disability.

Your child's special education services must be delivered in the least restrictive environment (LRE). This means that your child cannot be separated from non-handicapped students unless the nature and severity of his handicap is such the "education in regular classes with the use of supplementary aids and services cannot be achieved satisfactorily" (see Chapter 7, "School Option #1: Public Schools"). This decision is made at the IEP meeting, and you will be asked to either accept or reject the decision.

Reevaluation for special education students is every three years and the IEP is reviewed annually. However, you or your child's teacher can request a reevaluation more frequently.

If you reject the plan, you have the right to a free, independent evaluation paid for by the school system. However, the second evaluation must cover the same areas as the first evaluation given by the school system. While the second evaluation is being conducted, your child would remain in the current educational placement.

The law also established early intervention programs for children with developmental delays between birth to age 3. An amendment in 1991 expanded these services to include children between the ages of 3 to 5 who experience, or are at risk for, developmental delays. If you are concerned about your infant or toddler, contact your local school system to get further information about these services.

All information about your child is kept confidential. It cannot be released to anyone else without your written consent.

Understanding Due Process Under IDEA

Parents have the right to request a due process hearing if they disagree with their child's identification, evaluation or educational placement, or any aspect related to the provision of a free appropriate public education. A due process hearing involves an impartial third party — a hearing officer — who hears the evidence and issues a decision based upon that evidence and the requirements of the IDEA. The hearing is conducted by the State Educational Agency (SEA). The due process hearing must be completed and a copy of the decision mailed to parents and school officials within 45 days of the parents' request.

At this point, I would like to interject my own thoughts on due process. Although the hearing officer is paid by the school district, the officer is considered neither an employee of the school district nor connected with the school district involved in educating or caring for your child. The person must not have any personal or professional interest that might conflict with his or her objectivity in the hearing.

Families have filed for due process for a variety of reasons, from not following the IEP to failing to teach the child appropriately. And while due process has worked for some families, it has been disastrous for others. In cases that I have been made aware of, the families felt that the hearing officer was impartial, but, at the same time, each of the families agreed that, had they known what the hearing would entail, they would not have put themselves (and definitely not their child) through the process. Why?

A due process hearing is not just one or two school administrators and you with your child sitting down in front of a hearing officer. Instead, you have the school administration coming to the hearing with a battery of attorneys, and if the school is going to be represented by an attorney (or attorneys), then you had better have one, too. Thus, the hearing really turns into a court proceeding (which it technically is). Also, the due process hearing may only take a day to hear, but the beforehand maneuvers of depositions and the barrage of questions by both sides can be endless. As one parent said, it was an "interrogation" as if "I were on trial for murder."

If all that were not enough, once the due process hearing is filed, all professionals who have ever been involved with your child – teachers, school psychologist, counselors, etc. – are notified. In a sense, these professionals are also put "on trial" as they must defend their treatment, their teaching and their professionalism. When this happens, you, the parent, suddenly become the "school pest." Some families which I have known, who have filed for due process, have transferred their child out of the public school rather than have their child feel any humiliation or retaliation from the school. That is not to say that all schools retaliate. They do not. In fact, many times, the school will do just the opposite – work that much harder to find a compromise.

If you find that, after exhausting all other avenues, there is no reasonable solution or compromise, and you find that you are heading toward due process, then I have three pieces of advice:

– **Hire an Attorney.** Pick one who has experience in going up against a governmental agency, such as the school board, one who does not care if he or she is up against a governmental agency and one who has fought the school board on other issues, too. To find this attorney, you may have to go outside the area in which you live and maybe even out of state. You can contact your state LDA chapter or the na-

Compliance with Section 504

To be in compliance with Section 504, a school district must:

- Provide written assurance of nondiscrimination

- Designate an employee to coordinate compliance

- Provide grievance procedures to resolve complaints

- Provide notice of nondiscrimination in admission or access to its programs or activities. Notice must be included in a student/parent handbook

- Annually identify and locate all qualified children with disabilities who are not receiving a public education

- Annually notify persons with disabilities and their parents or guardians of the district's responsibilities under Section 504

- Provide parents or guardians with procedural safeguards, which include:

  - notice of their rights
  - an opportunity to review relevant records
  - an impartial hearing. Parents or guardians must be notified of their right to request a hearing regarding the identification, evaluation, or educational placement of persons with handicapping conditions.

tional chapter for a possible recommendation. But whatever you do, get an experienced attorney who understands
LD as well as the IDEA and/or Section 504.

– **Go to your attorney well-prepared.** That means you
should have the proper, complete documentation that will
be needed for due process (see Chapter 5, "Testing, Record-
Keeping and Parent/Teacher Conferences"). Without proper
documentation, you probably do not have a case, and if your
attorney is knowledgeable on LD, IDEA and/or Section 504,
the first thing they will tell you is that, without documentation, you don't have a case.

– **Be prepared to transfer your child out of the system**,
and maybe even other siblings, depending upon your relationship with the school and the school district. You do not
know how the school, the teacher(s) or the school district
may react – possibly helpfully, possibly not.

The point is that a due process hearing should only be
used as the last resort. Do not play around with threats, since
you could back yourself into a corner. Instead, take the time to
work with your school district, its administrative staff and, of
course, the personnel to whom your child is assigned. But if all
else fails, resort to due process. More importantly, remember
that your child is the focus – not your own feelings and egos.

Understanding Parents' Rights
Under the Law (IDEA)

It is important for parents of children with LD to understand their basic rights. Through understanding of the law,
parents can build their confidence to advocate for their child
more effectively. Remember, knowledge is power and under-

standing the law will ensure that your child is getting the educational placement and related services that your child needs.

And one more item – it is most important to become familiar with your state's special education law. IDEA is a *federal* law and, as such, provides *minimum* requirements that states must meet in order to receive federal funds to assist in providing special education and related services. Your state law and regulations may go beyond the federal requirements, and it is important to know their specifics, since each state has its own set of regulations. You may want to contact your State Department of Education (DOE), Office of Special Education, and ask for a parent handbook on special education.

Understanding Section 504

Section 504 of the Rehabilitation Act of 1973

Section 504 is the section of the Rehabilitation Act of 1973 that applies to persons with disabilities. Basically, it is a civil rights act which protects the civil and constitutional rights of persons with disabilities. Section 504 prohibits organizations which receive federal funds from discriminating against otherwise qualified individuals solely on the basis of handicap. Section 504 is enforced by the U.S. Department of Education, Office for Civil Rights (OCR).

According to the Learning Disabilities Association of America, Section 504 prohibits the following types of discrimination:

— Denial of the opportunity to participate in, or benefit from a service which is afforded non-handicapped students.
— Refusing to allow a student with an IEP the opportunity

to be on the honor roll.

– Denying credit to a student whose absenteeism is related to the disability.

– Refusing to dispense Ritalin to a student with Attention Deficit Disorder. A school cannot require parents to waive liability as a condition of giving medicine; however, it is wise to get your physician's prescription to back up medical accommodations (see Chapter 6, "ADD and ADHD").

– Provision of opportunity to participate in, or to benefit from a service which is not equal to that afforded others.

– Determining sports eligibility based on a student's grades without regard to the student's handicapping condition.

– Provision of aids, benefits or services which are not as effective as those provided to others. Equally effective means equivalent, not identical, and must afford an equal opportunity, not equal results (for example, placing a student with a hearing impairment on the front row instead of providing an interpreter).

– Provision of different or separate benefits or services unless such action is necessary to be effective (for example, separate classes, schools or facilities).

– Aiding or perpetuating discrimination by providing assistance to an organization that discriminates. (for example, sponsoring a student organization that excludes persons with disabilities)

– Denial of the opportunity to participate on a planning or advisory board because of an individual's handicapping condition.

– Otherwise limiting the enjoyment of any right, privilege, advantage or opportunity enjoyed by others.

— Selecting a site or location which effectively excludes persons with disabilities or subjects them to discrimination (for example, locating students with disabilities in inferior facilities due to a lack of classroom space).

Understanding the Rights of Parents of Children With Disabilities (Section 504)

1. Your child is entitled to a free, appropriate public education that meets the unique educational needs of your child.

2. You will be notified when the school wishes to evaluate your child, wants to change your child's educational placement, or refuses your request for an evaluation or a change in placement.

3. You may request an evaluation if you think your child needs special education or related services.

4. You will be asked by your school to agree in writing to the evaluation and initial special education placement for your child. Your consent is voluntary and may be withdrawn at any time.

5. You may obtain an independent, low-cost evaluation if you disagree with the outcome of the school's evaluation. The school district will supply you with the names of local testing centers.

6. You may request a reevaluation if you suspect your child's current educational placement is no longer appropriate. The school must reevaluate your child at least every three

years, but your child's educational program must be reviewed at least once during each calendar year.

7. You may have your child tested in the language he or she
    knows best. For example, if your child's primary language
    is Spanish, he or she must be tested in Spanish. Also, stu-
    dents who are hearing impaired have the right to an in-
    terpreter during the testing.

8. The school must communicate with you in your primary
    language. The school is required to take whatever action
    is necessary to ensure that you understand its oral and
    written communication, including arranging for an in-
    terpreter if you are hearing impaired or if your primary
    language is not English.

9. You may review all of your child's records and obtain
    copies of these records, but the school may charge you
    a reasonable fee for making copies. Only you, as par-
    ents, and those persons directly involved in the educa-
    tion of your child will be given access to personal
    records. If you think any of the information in your
    child's records is inaccurate, misleading or violates the
    privacy or other rights of your child, you may request
    that the information be changed. If the school refuses
    your request, you then have the right to request a hear-
    ing to challenge the questionable information in your
    child's records.

10. You must be fully informed by the school of all the rights
    provided to you and your child under the law. You may
    participate in the development of your child's Individual-
    ized Education Program (IEP) or, in the case of a child

under school age, the development of an Individualized Family Service Plan (IFSP). The IEP and IFSP are written statements of the educational program designed to meet your child's unique needs. The school must make every possible effort to notify you of the IEP or IFSP meeting and arrange it at a time and place agreeable to you. As an important member of the team, you may attend the IEP or IFSP meeting and share your ideas about your child's special needs, the type of program appropriate to meeting those needs, and the related services the school will provide to help your child benefit from his or her educational program.

11. You may have your child educated in the least restrictive school setting possible. Every effort should be made to develop an educational program that will provide the greatest amount of contact with children who are not disabled.

12. You may request a due process hearing to resolve differences with the school that could not be resolved informally.

Filing a Complaint (Section 504)

To file a complaint, contact your regional Office for Civil Rights (OCR) and speak to the person who understands the applications of Section 504 on education and use that person as your contact. Explain the situation, specify the issue and site the area of discrimination. OCR should then send a representative to investigate the complaint.

If you disagree with OCR's ruling, the Freedom of Information Act allows you to ask for a copy of the investigation

plan used by the OCR representative, a copy of the investigation report and a copy of the school's documents. If you do
not think that the investigation was a careful and thorough
examination of the issue of complaint or you believe the conclusions are wrong, write a letter of appeal saying you do not
agree with the "Letter of Finding" and state your reasons.

Understanding Procedural Due Process (Section 504)

Due process, as it applies to special education, describes
the legal procedures and requirements developed to protect
the rights of children, parents and school districts. In respect
to children suspected of having a disability, due process guar-
antees a free and appropriate public education in the least
restrictive educational setting. For parents, due process protects their rights to have input into the educational program
and placement of their child, and to exercise options in cases
of disagreement with the recommendations of the school district. For school districts, due process offers recourse in cases
of parent resistance to a request for evaluation, challenges to
an independent evaluation sought by parents at public expense, or unwillingness of parents to consent to the Committee on Special Education (CSE) recommendation.

The components of due process include such procedural
safeguards as the following:

Appropriate written notice to parents is required in the
following situations:

—   actions proposed by the CSE to evaluate the existence of
     a suspected disability

— meetings by the CSE to discuss the results of the evaluation to determine a suspected disability
— meetings to discuss the development of an individual educational plan
— proposed actions to review an individual educational plan
— proposed actions to reevaluate the child's classification or placement
— aging out notification for disabled children no longer eligible for tuition-free educational services

Written consent from parents is required in four specific situations:

— consent for an initial evaluation on a child not previously classified as having a disability
— consent allowing for the provisions recommended by the CSE with regard to classification and special education placement
— notification prior to providing services for the first time for a disabled child in a 12-month program
— prior to the disabled child's aging out of public education

Confidentiality of records is protected under due process. Confidentiality ensures that only educational institutions or agencies who have legitimate interest in the child's education will be permitted to see the records. Written consent from parents is required for the release of any information on their child other than the following:

— to staff members or school officials within the school district in which the child is a resident — who must have a legitimate interest in the child's education

–   to other school districts in which the disabled child may
    enroll. In this case, the parents are notified of the trans-
    fer of information, may request copies of the informa-
    tion sent and may contest through a hearing the content
    of the transferred information.
–   a surrogate parent must be assigned. In most cases the
    child with a suspected disability is represented by his or
    her parents at CSE meetings; however, if the parents are
    unknown or unavailable, or the child is a ward of the
    state, the CSE must determine if there is a need for the
    assignment of a surrogate parent to represent the child.
    When this happens, the board of education chooses a
    surrogate from a list of eligible individuals.

An impartial hearing is a procedure used to resolve dis-
agreements between parents and the school district. This procedure of due process can be utilized when:

–   a parent disagrees with a CSE recommendation
–   a parent disagrees with a board of education determination
–   the CSE fails to evaluate and recommend a program within
    30 days of the signed consent by the parents
–   the CSE fails to implement its recommendations within
    the 30-day requirement period
–   there is a failure on the part of the school district to ad-
    minister a triennial evaluation
–   there is a failure on the part of the school district to hold
    an annual review on a disabled child
–   parent or parents are unwilling to give consent for an
    evaluation
–   parents are unwilling to consent to the recommendations
    of the CSE concerning the classification or special educa-
    tion placement of a disabled child

If all else fails, appeals to your State Commissioner of Education provide another level of resolution for parents and school districts when an impartial hearing cannot resolve the disagreement. This is a legal process and the procedures are usually outlined in state manuals on the Commissioner's regulations.

Comparing the Laws

The following is a brief comparison of the two federal laws (IDEA and Section 504) developed by the Washington State Department of Education, reprinted by permission.

— Purpose —

IDEA: To provide federal financial assistance to state and local education agencies to assist them in educating children with disabilities.

Section 504: To eliminate discrimination on the basis of disability in all programs and activities receiving federal financial assistance.

— Who Is Protected —

IDEA: All school-age children who fall within one or more of 13 specific categories of disability and who, because of the disability, need special education and related services.

Section 504: All school-aged children who have a physical or mental impairment that substantially limits a major life activ-

---

REMEMBER

Schools which accept federal money must comply with *both* PL 94-142 (Individuals with Disabilities Education Act, IDEA) and Section 504 of the Rehabilitation Act of 1973. Compliance with IDEA does not necessarily mean that a district is in compliance with Section 504. One does not take precedence over the other.

---

ity, have a record of such an impairment, or are regarded as having such an impairment. Major life activities include walking, seeing, hearing, speaking, breathing, learning, working, caring for oneself and performing manual tasks.

— Provide a Free and Appropriate Public Education —

IDEA: Requires FAPE be provided to only those protected students who, because of the disability, need special education or related services. Defines FAPE as special education and related services. Requires a written IEP document with specific content and a required number of specific participants at the IEP meeting.

Section 504: Requires that FAPE be provided to only those protected students who, because of a disability, need special education or related services. Defines FAPE as regular or special education and related aids and services. Does not require a written IEP, but does require a plan.

— Special Education versus Regular Education —

IDEA: A student is protected by IDEA if, and only if, because of a disability, the student needs special education.

Section 504: A student is protected by Section 504 regardless of whether the student needs special education.

— Funding —

IDEA: Provides additional funding for protected students.

Section 504: Does not provide additional funds.

— Procedural Safeguards —

IDEA: Requires written notice and specific content to be included in the notice. Requires written notice prior to any change in placement.

Section 504: Does not require written notice. Requires notice prior to any "significant change" in placement.

— Evaluation —

IDEA: Requires informed consent before an initial evaluation is conducted. Requires reevaluation at least every three years. A reevaluation is not required before a change in placement. Provides for independent educational evaluation at district expense if parent disagrees with evaluation obtained by school and if the hearing officer concurs.

Section 504: Requires informed consent before an initial evaluation is conducted. Requires periodic reevaluations. Requires reevaluation before a significant change in placement. No provision for independent evaluations at district expense.

— Educational Plan —

IDEA: An IEP is required for students.

Section 504: An Accommodation Plan is used which is not as detailed as an IEP.

— Placement Procedures —

IDEA: An IEP meeting is required before any change in placement.

Section 504: A reevaluation meeting is required before any "significant change" in placement.

— Due Process —

IDEA: Contains detailed hearing rights and requirements.

Section 504: Requires notice, the right to inspect records, to participate in a hearing and be represented by counsel, and a review procedure.

— Enforcement —

IDEA: Enforced by the U.S. Office of Special Education Programs.
Section 504: Enforced by the U.S. Office for Civil Rights.

I would imagine by now you may feel a little overwhelmed, but, again, you are not alone. It takes time to accept that your child is LD, and before you can fully accept it, the school district and other professionals are throwing terminology at you, presenting options, and now I am throwing out legalese. The best advice I can give you is to form a partnership with your school, the administration, the teacher and other professionals to find the best placement for your child.

In a Nutshell . . .

— IDEA is a federal law that includes all school-age children who, because of the disability, need special education and related services.
— Section 504 is also a federal law, and it deals with the civil rights of the disabled.
— The IEP is the "heart and soul" of IDEA, and, as parents, you need to understand the makeup of the IEP and its relevance.
— Each state also has its own laws in addition to the *minimum* by the federal law. So check with your state Department of Education and familiarize yourself with your state's regulations.
— Threats only intimidate, so try to work with the school district, teachers and other professionals first before resorting to due process.

Frequently Asked Questions Concerning the Law

Is every child in every public school entitled to an IEP?

No, but that would not be a bad idea, since the IEP is a written education plan for the child who is LD. Also, remember that the IEP is mandated through the federal law, IDEA. If it were not mandated, I doubt seriously if school systems would require an IEP for the child with LD due to economics, time requirements and paperwork.

Can I, as a parent, recommend accommodations which will help my child in the classroom?

Absolutely! In fact, the special education team should encourage you to make recommendations. Remember that you, as parents, know your child better than any professional, so speak up and work with the professionals in finding the best goals and accommodations for your child. Also, note that if the accommodations are not written in the IEP, the school *does not* have to make the accommodations.

Can I include the use of a computer for my child's use in the classroom?

Yes, but make sure your request is in the IEP or it may never happen. Remember, if it is in the IEP, then the school will be required to get a computer in your child's classroom. Also, when requesting, make sure a time request is also made. For instance, allow your child the use of the computer for word processing or for taking tests, or for work at least 30 minutes a day, three days a week. Request exactly what you want, because if it is not spelled out in the IEP, it probably will never happen.

As a parent, do I have to attend the IEP meeting?

No, but as a parent you are a member of the team of professionals that will develop and write an IEP for your child. If you cannot attend, find someone in your family to attend who is genuinely interested in your child's well-being.

Does IDEA change from state to state?

No. IDEA is a federal law, so it is uniform throughout our country. However, in addition to the federal law, each state will have its own set of laws governing children with LD. So check your state Department of Education (DOE) to find out which laws govern children with LD.

What is the major difference between Section 504 of the Rehabilitation Act of 1973 and IDEA?

Both laws are federal, but the difference is that Section 504 is more of a civil rights bill that eliminates discrimination, whereas IDEA provides federal assistance to state and local education agencies to assist them in educating children with disabilities. There are several more differences which are explained in this chapter.

Can I request a second opinion on the psychoevaluation testing?

Yes. If you want a second opinion, you have the right under IDEA to a free, independent evaluation paid for by the school system. Because of economics, the school system may balk at the idea of having a second opinion, however, you are protected under IDEA to request a second opinion. Remember, though, the second evaluation must cover the same areas as the first evaluation given by the school district.

See also "Suggested Reading" for Chapter 3, pp. 271-72.

Chapter 4

The Role of
the Family

Understanding Household Fatigue

A child who is LD, whether mildly or severely, strains the whole family. Pressures of rearing any child can often create disharmony in the happiest of homes. Added to those problems a child with LD or ADD or ADHD or all three disorders, and I guarantee not only will there be disharmony but also an incredible amount of chaos and stress. However, this situation can be controlled to a certain extent or at the very least kept to a minimum.

The disharmony magnified by the stress level of the family is also known as "household fatigue." Parents today are tired. As parents, we mediate, plan, referee, advocate, intervene on behalf of all our children and, in particular, our child with LD. We also provide the emotional support for the child with LD and balance the remaining energy and attention to other family members.

Understanding Mother's Stress

When a child has LD, the entire family is affected. A family can easily double the work load when caring for a child with LD — stress is usually at an all-time high and patience is in short supply! Mothers are often the most involved with day-to-day activities and issues, and many times are the main contact with the school and the teacher. The mothers are the ones who usually (but not always — I heartily acknowledge single fathers and househusbands) attend the parent/teacher conferences and join and attend the school's parent or booster club. They are the ones who drop their child off in the morning and pick up the child in the afternoon, talk with the teacher in person or via phone, take the child to the doctor, ballet lessons, or to Little League. Most often, it is the mother who listens when the child is hurt, referees among other siblings and takes charge of the day-to-day activities of running a household. At the same time the mother is balancing home life, she is also caring for a child with LD and possibly building a career outside the home. No wonder mothers are tired!

Understanding Father's Stress

By virtue of their traditional role as primary caretaker for the family, the mother forces herself to recognize the reality of her child's disability. The father, on the other hand, does not spend as much time with his children since he usually does not attend school and medical appointments or after-school activities. As a result, it takes the father more time to adjust to the fact his child is LD, and he may pretend for a long time that the situation is less severe than it really is. However, the father should be involved, and it may take the mother to help the father accept the fact their child is LD by keeping the father informed of all medical, educational and social scenarios. Only when the father becomes directly part of the educational team will he become more supportive. Many times, becoming involved helps a father to overcome guilt, grief and/or denial. Once he is involved, he will often want a more direct role in his child's growth, development and educational goals.

The effect of both parents' efforts and involvement in any child's social well-being and educational goals cannot be underestimated. However, dual involvement for parents with children with LD is *essential*. Activities which cause normal stress in most homes cause an extraordinary level of stress in homes of children with LD.

Understanding Stressful Circumstances

Homework is just one of the many stressful issues faced by all families. Because the simplest assignment can turn into a nightmare for the child with LD, the entire family can get caught up in the turmoil. Most children with LD work extra hard in school just to keep up with their classmates, especially if they are part of inclusion (see Chapter 1, "Identification, Diagnosis and Acceptance"). When they return home after the usual stressful day at school, they are expected to sit down and work some more. These children are tired and so are the parents. The result is more stress in an already-stressed family. Many times, the homework never gets done, or the parents, in an effort to keep the frustration level low, will help

How Parents Can Help Their Children With Homework

Set up a homework schedule

For some children, the responsibility of deciding when to sit down and do homework may be too difficult. Children with LD and ADHD need structure and structure includes a definite time to do homework. And once the time is determined, the schedule should be adhered to as closely as possible.

Rank assignments

For children with LD, and ADHD in particular, this is especially important. Without some parental help, these children may dwell over this choice for a long period of time, because everything takes on the same level of importance. Ranking assignments means that the parent determines the order in which the assignments are completed. Do not watch over or sit beside your child while he or she does homework. Employing this technique may create learned helplessness because the same "assistance" is not imitated in the classroom. However, children with LD or ADHD sometimes need parents to check on their progress from time to time.

Never let homework drag on all evening

For the child with LD, and especially ADD/ADHD, the child needs to see an end to the homework. If you allow homework to drag on hour after hour with very little performance, increased feelings of inadequacy and the child's self-esteem will suffer. If this occurs, end the work period after a reasonable period of time and write the teacher a note explaining the circumstances.

Check correct problems first

When your child brings you a paper to check, mention to him or her how well he or she did on the correct problems, spelling words, or other work. This helps with self-esteem and the child will be more willing to correct the incorrect answers. For those which are incorrect say, "I bet if you go back and check these over you may get a different answer."

continued on the next page

continued from the previous page

Discuss homework questions before your child reads the chapter

Discuss the questions to be answered *before* the child reads the chapter. In this way, he or she will know what important information to look for while reading.

Check small groups of problems at a time

The child with LD can benefit greatly from immediate gratification. If you child is having difficulty, for example, with math, then have your child do only five problems at a time then come to you to check them. Additionally, if the child is doing the assignment incorrectly, the error can be detected and explained, preventing the child from doing the entire assignment incorrectly.

Place textbook chapters on tape

For the child who has an auditory deficit, or for the child who is an auditory learner, placing a chapter on tape is a godsend. Also, textbooks are available through school districts and local library but you need to call for information on how to obtain the textbooks. Research indicates that the more sensory input children receive, the greater the chance the information will be retained. Whether your child is LD or not, parents can help their children by placing science or social studies chapters on tape so that the child can listen while reading along.

Avoid finishing assignments for your child

Many times, parents – because they are tired or they feel sorry for their child with LD or just for some peace and quiet in the home – may complete the homework assignment rather than the child doing it. If children cannot complete an assignment, and they have honestly tried, write the teacher a note explaining the circumstances.

Check homework assignments at the end of the evening

This will reduce the child's concerns over the thought of bringing incorrect homework to school. It also offers children a feeling of accomplishment, a source of positive attention and a sense of security that the work is complete.

or finish the homework assignment. Meanwhile, siblings finish their homework assignments quickly and easily. Resentment, frustration, chaos and stress fill the household.

Another fallout from household fatigue is divorce. A disability in a family, either physical, mental or emotional, causes the divorce rate among these families to increase significantly. Marital stress is normal and universal in families with a handicapped child. Parents should not feel defeated or even surprised at experiencing it. The relationship frequently is burdened by the stresses and strains of parenting the child with LD. These adults should seek help from a marriage counselor. A counselor is frequently able to help parents come to terms with their feelings and help them achieve the open communication they need to be emotional partners instead of antagonists. Husbands and wives should not be embarrassed to ask for help. It is a sign of strength to do so (Simon 27).

Understanding Sibling Rivalry

"He hit me"; "He's a retard"; "She broke my toy"; "She is driving me crazy!" These phrases from the siblings of and a child with LD could simply mean, "Why don't you spend time with me?" Sibling conflict is hard on the entire family.

Siblings are caught between two worlds: the outside world and the world at home. These two worlds place very different demands on siblings, and they want to do well and be loved in both. Outside the home, a premium is placed on normalcy. All children want to be as much like other children as possible. They want their families to be as much like other families, too. *Within* the family, however, children want almost the opposite. They want to stand out — to feel special in their parents' eyes. Having to compete with a brother or sister who really is "special" is difficult, and it makes them understandably jealous and resentful (Simon 34).

Brothers and sisters bounce between jealousy and embarrassment. Having to explain to their friends their brother's or sister's inappropriate remarks or behavior is hard for any child to do. They love their brother or sister dearly but cannot understand why they say and do embarrassing things in front of their friends. And their friends, not understanding what LD is, cannot understand a person who is LD. Parents need to look at situations from a child's point of view. Remember how normalcy was important when you were their age? Try to minimize their embarrassment.

Two things make children different from adults in their reactions to brothers or sisters with LD. One is their lack of information. Reading this book will give parents valuable information about their child's disability. Knowledge will help you understand and deal with the disability. Look for books that will help them, too. They often are too young and inexperienced to understand their sibling's problem. And to make matters worse, many times siblings believe they will "catch" it. Secondly, children "act out" — they behave badly to get attention. Adults have learned to deal with negative feelings in socially acceptable ways. For children, however, bad behavior is sometimes the only way they know to get the attention they feel they need.

Children can be taught to cope in a number of ways. Talking to them when they act out can help them deal with their feelings. Parents need to explain their own feelings. Modeling good communication skills can teach children to recognize and express their own feelings. Talking is not always easy, though. Older children may be afraid to tell parents their feelings for fear of hurting them or adding to their burden. Younger children may be unable or unwilling to express emotions.

Even when siblings do talk, the things they say may not be pleasant for parents to hear. Parents want all their children to grow up healthy, happy and tolerant. Children who resent having a brother or sister who is LD or hate the embarrassment he or she creates in and outside the home, threaten the goals of family health and harmony. Parents of LD children sometimes forget that all kids — even those in *normal* families — go through periods of hating each other.

Parents are continually being told by their other children: "You never let *me* get away with that!" or "Why should he or she get *all* the attention?" or, in my case, "You spoil Dan too much." Sometimes parents need to explain, again, why the child with LD is having so much difficulty. It is true that sometimes for peace, quiet and some sanity in the house, the child with LD gets away with something he or she should not. Inevitably, this brings out the sibling rivalry in full force.

Brothers and sisters can usually get their revenge on their sibling with LD at report card time. Report card days are especially unpleasant for the child with LD. Comparisons are not unusual, and because the child with LD does not come out on top, resentment is the end result. The frustration level becomes almost too much to bear for both child and parent.

Emotional dependence upon parents by the child with LD is another problem area. Sometimes parents come to rely on that dependence for their own fulfillment. Caring for the child who is LD has become their main work and the center of their lives. Such parents have to learn to wrest themselves away from their child, just as the child has to carve out a separate identity and establish an independent life (Smith 150).

As painful as it is, parents of children with LD frequently must watch them being teased and *not* take action. The job of parents is to help children find the tools to handle such situations — themselves. Parents have to watch their children fall and fail and pick themselves up again. If parents absorb too many of the bumps and bruises, their children do no learn the skills that allow them to grapple with adversity (Smith 159).

Helping the Harried Family

What parents need to do is to listen carefully, to keep lines of communication open, to feel their child's feelings of rejection, failure, despair and humiliation without absorbing them. Part of separating from one's children is becoming detached from their anxieties and hurts. Parents hurt when their child hurts, but that must not become the parents' problem. Parents and teachers need to help empower children with LD so they can confront problems and seek ways to effectively deal with all the "bumps and bruises" that come their way.

Some solutions do exist to alleviate stress, household fatigue and sibling rivalry. First of all, parents need to ensure their own good mental health. Finding time to spend alone and with each other is a *must*. Carve out a few minutes at least once a week and, hopefully, several times a week, to do something *you* want to do — resting, reading a book, exercising, walking, meditating — can do wonders for the heart and soul and can certainly relieve some of the stress.

If your household is a two-parent household, share some of the more stress-related issues or chores. More importantly, you both must agree to support each other's decisions when dealing with all your children and, in particular, your child with LD. Do not try to compete as parents with your children's emotions!

Another stress-reducing idea is to hire a baby sitter. While you work one-on-one with one of the children, the baby sitter works with the other children. Of course, rotate the time during which each child spends the one-on-one time with you. Another idea is to have boys' day/night out and girls' day/night out once a week. Translation: Dad takes the boys, and mom takes the girls, and each parent plans an activity to do with the children. The reverse can also hold true with dad taking the girls and mom taking the boys. For example, since my family has two boys, each of us takes one of the boys on a special weekend trip – from skiing to backpacking. It is a father-son or a mother-son outing, and both of our boys look forward to doing something special with just their mom or dad.

You can drive yourself crazy trying to *do* everything for everyone, and, no matter how hard you try, it is impossible to *be* everything to everyone. When children complain that you are not being fair, try to remember the true meaning of the word *fair.* Fair is when everyone gets what he or she needs, not necessarily what he or she wants. No matter which way you look at the problem, children with LD have greater needs. It is that simple.

Let's face it, we all sometimes lose control! All parents have yelled at their child or used words which were later regretted. Remember, you are not alone and certainly you are not an exception. We have all *lost it* at one time or another. You do, however, need to be willing to say "I am sorry" or "I made a mistake."

Every family's level of tolerance for conflict is different. When conflict begins to escalate, it is time to talk to someone. If you catch the situation early enough, the intervention does not have to be long term – brief therapy or therapy during certain stages of development can be very helpful. If you or any member of your family begin to feel out of control, seek professional help. Remember, it is easier to get the situation *under control* before it gets *out of control.* If you are worried about paying for this kind of help, check with your community mental health agencies. Most have sliding-scale fees based on income and many insurance companies cover this type of service. Therapy is essential when your life is out of control.

Disciplining the Child With LD

Disciplining your child with LD can be just as stressful as sibling rivalry. Simply put, children with LD need structure. Children, whether LD or not, need realistic, fair and well-defined limits and guidelines. They need to know the expectations and the consequences. It is not enough to tell them what the rules are; the consequences for breaking the rules must be clearly stated. Sometimes it may be necessary show them how to follow the rules set down.

Many children with LD need extra time to follow directions. They often get angry if they are expected to jump at a moment's notice to do a chore. Give your child a time line and make sure he or she understands *what* is expected and *when* it is expected. Children with LD usually do not plan ahead. A time line will give ample warning when you want them to do something. I not only give my son a time line, but I also tell him, usually at the beginning of the day, just what I expect from him during the day and advise him of the time frame. This way, Dan can plan his day too, sprinkled with what I have requested. By giving a time line and explaining what you want done and when you expect it to be done, you are giving your child a chance to plan time for both work and play.

In addition to time lines, contracts are a wonderful source to use to reinforce positive behavior or achieve success. Contracts should state, in clear and understandable language, the reasonable goals and expectations to which both you and your child can agree. If you use contracts, make sure that both you and your child write the contract, sign the agreement and stick to the terms.

Spend time focusing on what goes well. Parents are often so consumed by all the things which need to get corrected that we forget to stop and congratulate ourselves and our children when something goes well. If you make an effort to catch your child doing something well, you may not need to dole out so much discipline. Punishment tells children what not to do, but rewards tell children what behavior is acceptable. If long-term changes in behavior are desired, then rewards must be included. Rewards need not be money, they can include verbal praise, written notes of thanks, extended play or television time or any other special treat you can think of that would be a reward for your child.

When disciplining a child with LD, try to use phrases such as "poor judgment," "inappropriate behavior," "lapse of memory," or "acting before thinking." Focusing on the *act* rather than on the personality allows the child with LD to save face.

If one parent disagrees with the other parent's punishment, try to discuss it at a private moment. Open disagreement concerning a disciplinary action can sometimes confuse the child, and the child can then turn the punishment into an argument between parents while the child gets off the hook. The most important thing to remember with discipline is that a parent begins it, and the parent ends it. In too many situations, the parent begins the discipline, but sympathy for the child, manipulation by the child or inconsistency of the parent prevents closure.

When you have lost your patience and you are openly angry, delay punishment for 15 minutes or, if necessary, overnight. Give yourself and your child a cooling-off period. Sometimes your stress level is on overload or the outrageous behavior has you so angry and upset that you may say or do something that you may regret later. Use the phrase "I am so angry or upset that I do not want to deal with this situation. So go to your room, and I will deal with you in fifteen minutes (or tomorrow morning)." The use of delay will reduce impractical consequences.

Finally, pick and choose your arguments. Do not ignore misbehavior or irresponsibility just because the child is LD. On one hand, constantly nagging or calling attention to minor mishaps will only deflate his or her self-esteem. However, children with LD cannot get off the hook for poor judgment because they are LD. *Remember, LD is a disorder not an excuse.*

Finding Outside Support

Do not wait until you are at your wit's end to go for advice or help. Many wonderful parent support groups across the country help parents cope with the child with LD. Support groups are available for both the child with LD and his/her siblings.

Small support groups for adults as well as children offer the nurturing environment conducive to comforting and supporting parents, children with LD and their siblings. Children often will listen to other parents before they will listen to their own parents. Siblings need an outlet where they can talk to others their own age about the problems they have experienced having a brother or sister with LD. The child with LD needs an outlet, too, where he or she can meet and talk to other children with LD.

Support groups usually try to fill the individual's need,

Selected Organizations for Exceptional Children

**American Speech-Language
Hearing Association**
10801 Rockville Pike
Rockville, MD 20852

**Association for Children with
Retarded Mental Development**
902 Broadway
New York, NY 10010

**Attention Deficit Disorder
Association (A.D.D.A.)**
8091 South Ireland Way
Aurora, CO 80016
(A national alliance of ADHD support groups
that provides referrals and information to
parents and parent support groups).

**CHADD - Children and Adults
with Attention Deficit Disorder**
499 Northwest 70th Avenue, Ste. 308
Plantation, FL 33317
(A national alliance of parent organizations
that provides information and support to
parents of children with ADD/ADHD).

**Chicago Institute for
Learning Disabilities**
University of Illinois at Chicago Circle
Box 4348
Chicago, IL 60680
(social adjustment, language)

Council for Exceptional Children
1920 Association Drive
Reston, VA 22091
(CEC division for Learning Disabilities is involved in improving the quality of services
to children, youth and adults who are LD).

**Learning Disabilities Association
of America (LDA)**
4156 Library Rd.
Pittsburgh, PA 15234
Phone (412) 341-1515, (412) 341-8077

(LDA is an international membership organization of parents of children with LD,
and professionals who are devoted to
finding solutions to problems associated
with LD).

**National Information Center for
Children and Youth
with Disabilities (NICHCY)**
PO Box 1492
Washington, DC 20013-1492
Phone (800) 999-5599
(NICHCY is an information clearinghouse
that provides free information on disabili-
ties and disability-related issues serving
ages birth to age 22).

Orton Society, Inc.
8415 Bellona Lane
Baltimore, MD 21204
Phone (410)296-0232
(The goals of the society are to improve understanding and knowledge about dyslexia
and to promote research and appropriate
teaching techniques).

**Sibling Support Project (Sibshops)
Children's Hospital and
Medical Center**
CL-09 / P.O. Box 5371
Seattle, WA 98105-0371
Phone (206)368-4911
Project Director: Donald Meyer
E-Mail:dmeyer@chmc.org
For information and newsletter contact:

The Sibling Information Network
911 Main Street, Suite 3A
East Hartford, CT 06108
(203)282-7050
 Internet access:
http://www.chmc.org/departmt/sibsupp
(Sibshops is a nationwide program of workshops for siblings of children with special
needs, ages 8-13).

share information, lend a shoulder to cry on or just provide someone to talk to. Support groups vary. If your county has one of the recognized groups listed on the facing page, attend a meeting or two, and if you feel the support group meets your needs, then join it. If your community is too small for a support group then form one with a neighboring community. You will be surprised at what a support group can do for you, your child and other members of the family.

And one last point for all family members to remember: you do **NOT** have an LD child, an LD brother or an LD sister, you have a child with LD, a brother with LD or a sister with LD. There is a **BIG** difference! A child is *first* a child (or a sister or brother) who just happens to have a learning disability.

In a Nutshell . . .

— When a child has LD, the entire family is affected.
— Fair is when everyone gets what he or she needs, not necessarily what he or she wants.
— You need to be willing to say "I am sorry" or "I made a mistake."
— Every family's level of tolerance for conflict is different.
— If your family is in a situation where the degree of conflict is escalating, it is time to talk to someone. Get the situation under control *before* it gets out of control.
— Pick and choose your arguments.
— LD is a disorder, not an excuse.
— There *is* a difference between an LD child and a child with LD.

Frequently Asked Questions
Concerning the Role of the Family

How can I eliminate the stress that
my child with LD seems to cause?

Stress is common, whether or not you have a child with LD, ADD or ADHD. However, having a child with a disability usually adds a little more stress, but don't just blame it on your child with LD. You probably can never entirely overcome stress, but you can reduce it. First, try to figure out just what causes some of the more stressful times in your household, such as homework time, cleaning the house, cooking, getting ready for baths and bed. What time is most stressful? Once you can answer that, try to figure out what can be done to make the situation less stressful. For example, if bedtime seems to be filled with chaos, you might want to establish a quiet time, about 30 minutes before lights out, during which everyone — including parents — are sitting and reading quietly or reading to the children. Just keep working with various plans until one idea works better than others.

Is there any way to stop the name calling that seems
rather constant in our family?

Probably not. It goes on at school, too, so there is no reason to believe it will stop at home. Sibling rivalry has been going on since the beginning of the family. However, keep in mind that children, even those in the so-called "normal" families that you may wish you had, go through periods of hating one another or teasing those they love. And, also, as a parent, you cannot be with your child with LD 24 hours a day, so you must allow them the opportunity to work things out for themselves.

Being teased is painful, and not being able to take action is even more painful, but that is what you must teach your child — to advocate for himself or herself. There are a few books to help with this dilemma. See page 272-73 in the Suggested Reading section of this book.

What suggestions do you have for parents in relieving stress?

Before the parents can reduce the stress in their families, they must make sure that their stress level is under control. Take time for one another and for yourselves, individually. How can you dictate self-control if you are not in control yourself? At least once a week, do something for yourself — take a long walk, bike ride, read a book, get a facial, have a manicure or something that relaxes you. Then you and your partner take time for one another — dinner alone, a walk in the park — something that will relax both of you. Remember, keeping yourself healthy, physically and emotionally, is essential to your well being as well as that of your child and your family.

How can support groups help?

Support groups are just what they say they are — there to support you! Support groups try to fill the individual needs as well as share information, network, lend a shoulder to cry on, and, if nothing else, you will find other parents to talk to. Groups of parents can empathize with your concerns, give you new ideas for coping and provide comfort during the tough times. Support groups are always looking for members, so if you find a group that does not meet your needs, look at other support groups in your area for help.

*Homework time seems to be the most stressful time in
our house. How can we reduce the stress level?*

During homework, separate the children and try to work with
each child, guiding them through their homework assignments, even if it is only for a short time. Another idea is to
divide up the homework into 20- to 30-minute segments with
10- to 15-minute breaks between each segment. If you do take
breaks, though, make sure each child returns to the homework session in a timely manner.

See also "Suggested Reading" for Chapter 4, pp. 272-73.

Chapter 5

Testing, Record Keeping and Parent/Teacher Conferences

One of the worst mistakes a parent can make is not understanding test results and being afraid to ask questions of the psychologist for fear of sounding dumb. I made that mistake. As a result of my ignorance, I am including a chapter on testing as well as record keeping and conferences. All three topics are not only important but necessary if you want to become more knowledgeable about LD and become an advocate for your child.

Understanding the Tests

As was pointed out in Chapter 1, "Identification, Diagnosis and Acceptance", a psychoeducational evaluation is a series of tests used to determine if your child has a learning disability, and, if so, the nature of the disability. The importance of such testing cannot be underestimated. Without knowledge of the extent and kind of disability, we as parents cannot cope with or advocate for our children with LD. I know that the thought that your child might test LD is a terrifying one. It is even more terrifying to wait for the test results. However, it is better to know what your child's strengths and weaknesses are so you can also share this information with your child's teachers. This information will allow the school and teacher make the needed modifications and accommodations to help your child learn. You will be asked for permission, in writing, before the evaluation can take place and all test results are confidential. While you are waiting for the test results, remember the psychoeducational evaluation is not just one test but a series of tests that determine the learning disability.

The psychoeducational evaluation covers four areas of testing. The psychologist, tester or specialist who administers these tests should choose a minimum of two tests in each category. Since there are hundreds of tests to choose from, I will list and briefly describe the more commonly used tests in each area. Many of the tests will have several subtests, but not all subtests are given. The tester will decide which will be given and in what order.

Understanding Aptitude Tests

Aptitude is one of the first areas that will be tested. Aptitude is the natural ability, capacity or talent in a particular area, such as music or science. Aptitude is a specialized facility to learn or to understand a particular skill. Five tests are popular in this area:

Wechsler Intelligence Scale for Children, Revised (WISC-R)
(Ages: 6-17 years)

The most widely used individual intelligence tests in education are the Wechsler Scales. There are three Wechsler Scales which can be administered on subject areas appropriate for students from age 4 ½ to adult.

The Wechsler test measures general intelligence and is divided into two parts: verbal and performance. There are three scores: verbal, performance and a total score. The individual subtests in each part can provide information about specific strengths and weaknesses as well as attention factors. Once your child has finished taking the IQ portion and receives a score, the tester will use a formula to determine whether that score is truly reflective of his or her potential ability or is an underestimate of that ability. The difference between performance and ability can be caused by emotional factors, processing problems and neurological factors, to name a few. However, the important information the psychologist should give you is the significance of the gap. The tester should be able to give you, in layman's terms, a direct, nonmedical answer. If the tester does not clearly explain the results to you, keep asking questions until you understand their significance.

Woodcock-Johnson Psychoeducational Battery-Revised:
Tests of Cognitive Ability
(Grades: Preschool through adult)

This test is composed of 27 subtests which measure cognitive abilities (intelligence), scholastic aptitude and achievement. The first section measures cognitive abilities. These include long- and short-term memory, processing speed of visual and auditory information, understanding of information, and the ability to shift from one task to another. The scholastic aptitude measures aptitude in the academic skills. The last section is the achievement section which measures reading, math, written language and knowledge.

The Stanford-Binet Intelligence Scale:
Fourth Edition
(Ages: 2 years through adult)

This test studies the development of cognitive skills and helps differentiate between children who have a mental disability and those who have a specific learning disability. The test also helps teachers and psychologists understand why a particular child is having trouble learning in school, and it can help in the identification of gifted children.

The Stanford-Binet is an individual general intelligence test, and results can be interpreted in several ways, including verbal comprehension, nonverbal reasoning/visualization, and memory. The examiner asks the student to answer questions or perform tasks which assess a variety of abilities, including vocabulary, memory, abstract reasoning, numerical concepts, visual-motor skills, and social competence.

The Slosson Intelligence Test-Revised (SIT-R)
(Ages: 4 years through adult)

This test is a quick measure of intelligence and relies heavily on language. It tests general knowledge, comprehension, arithmetic, similarities and differences, vocabulary, and auditory memory, and it can be administered in 30 minutes. The Slosson was designed as a screening test to provide useful information about a student's *probable* level of mental ability. Although it can identify students in need of more intensive intellectual assessment, under no circumstances should it be substituted for the in-depth intellectual assessment needed for such critical educational decisions as class placement, retention or acceleration. In other words, do not allow a tester to use this one test to determine your child's intellectual ability.

Kaufman Assessment Battery for Children (K-ABC)
(Ages: 2½ to 12½)

The Kaufman is an individually administered test of mental processes and achievement. It contains 16 subtests and the actual test is very similar to the Woodcock-Johnson Psycho-Educational Battery, because it combines measures of intellectual ability and achievement in the same test. Do not allow the tester to use only this test as an IQ test.

Understanding Achievement Tests

The next area of testing concerns achievement. Achievement tests are designed to assess what a student has learned in relation to other students of the same age and grade level. The tests measure specific types of achievement in academic fields, such as math, reading, language, social studies and science. The *Woodcock-Johnson Psychoeducational Battery-Revised* and the *Wechsler Individual Achievement Test* can both be used to test achievement, in addition to the following specialized achievement tests:

Tests of Written Language-3 (TOWL-3)
(Ages: 7 years through 17)

One of the few standardized assessments of students' written language skills, this test uses an essay format as well as an objective answer format to get an understanding of how a child organizes information so he/she can write it down. The areas measured include vocabulary, thematic maturity (essay/theme composition), handwriting, spelling, word usage, style and grammar. If your child is given this test, be sure to ask to see the essay that your child wrote. It can be a real eye opener in understanding where and how severe the disability may be.

Woodcock Reading Mastery-Revised
(Grades: Kindergarten through 12th)

This test is a battery of five individually administered reading subtests. This test measures a wide range of reading skills. Subtests include letter identification, word identification, word attack, word comprehension and passage comprehension. All items on the tests require a verbal response; multiple-choice and yes-or-no items are not included.

Wide Range Achievement Test—R (WRAT-R)
(Ages: 5 years through adult)

A relatively quick test of reading, spelling and math. This test provides a grade score but does not provide diagnostic or remedial information. The reading section measures the ability to recognize letters and words. It does not measure comprehension. The procedure for this test is for the student to write dictated spelling words and write the answers to printed arithmetic problems. This test is usually given when time is a factor or as an indicator that more extensive testing is needed. Do not allow the tester use only this test as an achievement test. It needs to be used with other achievement tests.

Understanding Information-Processing Tests

The next area of testing concerns information processing, sometimes called intellectual processing. Tests for information processing measure how effectively students process, retain and express information that they receive through their physical senses, such as hearing and seeing.

Detroit Tests of Learning Aptitude
(Ages: 3 years to 10 or 6 years to 19)

The Detroit provides a broad sampling of a student's mental processes and specific intellectual, perceptual and cognitive functions. The test contains 19 tests which measure intelligence, language, attention and motor abilities. It assesses how a child processes information, how a child's attention level affects performance, and how written responses enhance or inhibit ability to perform.

Also included in the category of information-processing tests would be the previously mentioned *Woodcock-Johnson Psychoeducational Battery-Revised: Test of Cognitive Ability* and *Wechsler Intelligence Scale for Children, Revised (WISC-R)*.

In addition to the above-mentioned areas of testing (intelligence, aptitude, achievement and information processing) other assessment measures and factors should be used in determining the disability, class placement and retention. As mentioned in Chapter 1, a learning styles inventory will probably take place, as well as a developmental social assessment. The specialist who does the social assessment will interview *you* to find out such things as what age your child began to talk and walk, gain weight and other information that you may have forgotten but which could possibly be found in your child's baby book. So you may want to thumb through the pages of your child's baby book to jog your memory prior to the interview. Also, several questions may deal with your pregnancy and family history on both sides of the family, as well as your observations over the years with your child. You may find these questions rather personal, but they are necessary to ensure all factors in your child's life will be taken into consideration.

Understanding Physical Ability Tests

Other tests may be necessary in the area of physical ability such as: speech, language and hearing, as well as evaluations by specialists in physical therapy and occupational therapy. Speech and language therapists or pathologists examine a child's ability to understand language and the ability to express thoughts. They also look at how well the child speaks, based on the sounds that he or she should be able to pronounce according to age. If necessary, a hearing test may also be scheduled. The importance of speech and language testing cannot be underestimated. If your child cannot hear or understand the spoken word, he or she will not perform well on the other tests or understand and follow oral instructions. A physical therapist (PT) will test for gross motor skills, muscle tone and balance, and an occupational therapist (OT) will test for fine motor skills. OT testing is not routinely given unless there are extreme concerns about the way a child's nerves and muscles work together.

Many behaviors will be observed when a child is tested. Tests are samples of behavior, and scores may be adversely affected by student anxiety and fatigue or by emotional state. Since cooperation and motivation play such critical roles, testers should not rely on test scores alone to assess a child's performance but must consider test score results in relation to other indicators (Harwell 28). An appropriate placement can be recommended only after the analysis of all relevant tests, assessments, interviews and observations.

Keeping Up With Record Keeping

Record keeping is no one's favorite task, but if you have a child with LD, it is very important to keep your child's records from year to year in an orderly fashion. Now you are thinking, "My gosh my son is thirteen, and I have to organize the last thirteen years of reports." Well, believe it or not, it can be done easily and without a lot of heartburn.

First of all, you probably already have quite a few copies of some of your child's records, such as notes from teachers, report cards and mid-semester reports, but you may also request permission to see *all* of your child's educational records. Write a letter to the person in charge of records at your school, which may be the registrar or a guidance counselor. If you do not know the person in charge of records, call the school and ask the secretary or principal. State that you want to look at *all* of your child's records. Be sure to ask *where* all the records are kept. Many times, records are kept in several places, so be prepared to take down addresses and phone numbers. Then call and make an appointment with each contact.

Before you go to the school to review your child's records, take a few days, hours or minutes to organize the records you already have in your possession. The first step in untangling the records is to sort by school, year or any other general category or common thread that pulls all the records together. Eventually, you will want to keep the copies together from year to year and by school.

If possible, record the information you have on hand and take that information with you when you examine the schools' records. Then, as you review the records, list the names of the documents that you wish to copy. The school must allow you to see all of your child's records but may charge you for copies of the records.

I personally use a three-ring binder and divide the binder according to years. An expanding envelope file, available from an office supply store, can also be used. The first page of each year should contain the following information: 1] the name of the school, 2] teacher(s), 3] teacher's aide, 4] principal, 5] psychologist, and 6] any other adult that your child sees (or saw) on a regular basis. As I received reports and notes from the school and/or teacher, I entered them in the file or binder. When it is filled, write the dates covered (for example: "from 9/1/97 through 5/28/98") on the outside and begin another. Once you have caught up with your record keeping, then future record keeping will not be a problem, because you just add to your volume of material as you receive notes and reports from the school each year. (See the facing page for a list of records to keep.)

You need all possible records because we live in a very mobile society. Moves may include changing school districts, moving across county lines or moving to another state. If you keep your records in an orderly fashion, you will have a handle on what kind of teacher, schooling and what accommodations need to be made. Also, you may decide to look at other options in schooling (see Chapter 8, "School Option #2: Private Day and Boarding Schools") or use a private psychologist.

Well-ordered records will save you time and money if you

Records You Should Request and Keep

- copies of teachers' notes
- progress notes
- report cards
- late slips
- achievement scores
- a cumulative card or folder
- nurse's record
- discipline notes
- written correspondence
- assessment reports, such as the results of IQ and academic achievement tests (IQ tests are now commonly called *School Abilities Index)*
- group IQ tests (usually given in grades 3,6,9)
- physical or motor skill, speech and language, and social-emotional evaluations
- reports from medical doctors (vision, hearing, physical exams)
- notice of IEP meeting
- evaluation or assessment information presented at the IEP meeting
- copy of the actual IEP
- summary of the deliberations
- any other documents generated by the school or special education department

can present past testing information and correspondence to the professional you choose. Also, the time may come when you are forced to use due process (See Chapter 3, "The Law Is On Your Side") to make your school comply with the law. You will need all records, and, if you hire an attorney, the first things he or she will ask to see are all the records and correspondence. So, start now and get in the habit of saving every bit of information you can, since you never know just when or what you may need.

Keeping Unwritten Records

You must keep not only written communications but you must also keep a log of important phone calls, noting the date and time and summarizing the conversation. A spiral notebook kept at the telephone for just such calls and conversations is an excellent way to track the conversation. A spiral notebook allows you to doodle, scribble or cross out, but a spiral also enables you to show that you have not added or deleted anything. If writing is difficult for you, then, after the conversation, tape-record your mental notes from the conversation. Include the date and time and oral summary of the conversation. Failing that, tell the person the conversation is being taped and tape it.

You also need to keep notes on any other conversations or meetings with school officials and staff. Notes of conversations should include whether conversation was by phone or in person, the date, time of day, person(s) with whom you spoke, and it should include a brief summary of the discussion.

The next suggestion may be a little uncomfortable for you, but you should tape-record all IEP meetings and keep the tapes in the folder with the paper information. The participants in the IEP meeting may feel a little uncomfortable about being taped, but if they are true professionals who are sure of their material, they will not object to being taped. Remember, the IEP is probably the most important meeting and document that you keep on your child. So, tape it, even if the participants feel a little uncomfortable.

Filing Complaints for Noncompliance

If your school does not comply with letting you see, copy or correct records, you may send a written complaint to the Family Education Rights and Privacy Act (FERPA) office, which is responsible for enforcement of the Buckley Amendment. The Buckley Amendment gives parents of students under the age of 18 the right to see, make copies and correct their child's records. You must file your complaint as soon as possible after the refusal and, of course, keep a copy of your complaint letter. The address is:

FERPA Office
U.S. Department of Education
Room 4074, Switzer Building
400 Maryland Avenue, S.W.
Washington, DC 20202-6186

Record keeping is a fact of life. It is not something anyone relishes doing, but it is something that has to be done on a regular basis. Once you get into the habit, it will become second nature and not so much a chore. Besides, over the years it is interesting to look back over your notes just to see how much your child has matured and learned.

Handling Parent/Teacher Conferences

Your child is a reflection of *you* and that is why, when your child's teacher calls to set up an appointment to discuss your child's progress or behavior, you suddenly feel that you will also be on trial also. You feel your child's progress and behavior reflects how good a parent you have been. This is natural.

You probably receive phone calls from your child's teacher quite often, especially if the teacher does not have the slightest idea how to teach to the child with LD and/or ADD/ADHD. However, *before* the teacher calls you into the classroom, take the first step. Drop the teacher a note and ask for help solving a minor problem. For example, ask the teacher's advice on how to get your child to read more books for pleasure. This is especially helpful if your teacher is a specialist in reading, as many teachers of children with LD are. Or, ask the teacher for advice on teaching your child how to share.

You probably already have an answer to both of these questions, but it may help spark an interest from your child's teacher to focus more on your child. By contacting the teacher first, you are showing the teacher that you are concerned about your child's eduction, and, at the same time, you are establishing a more personal relationship with your child's teacher. More importantly, you are also creating the atmosphere that you want for all future conferences, meetings and phone calls, because you are attempting to work with your child's teacher in a non-hostile situation. Even if writing is not your forte, make the first effort in contacting the teacher.

A written note shows that you are concerned parents who care about their child's education. A written note also gives you and the teacher time to think before expressing or responding to an idea. The teacher must coordinate times with both parents and other teachers and professionals who may be involved in the conference.

Often your note will do the trick. Your thoughts may stimulate the teacher to try something or to suggest something you or your child can do. But sometimes the teacher may surprise you by viewing the problem differently and suggesting an "off-the-wall" solution. However, if you feel the teacher's response was inadequate or worse yet, ignored, it may be time for a face-to-face conference.

A major purpose of your conference is to share information about your child. When I attend a conference, I try to compose a list of topics which I want to discuss and take it to the conference for reference. Be sure to refer to problems as the *child's* problem and not the teacher's. If you place the blame on the teacher from the beginning, you are only backing the teacher into a defensive corner and, probably, no positive effect will come from the conference. You can also jot down possible solutions that the teacher could try. But again, use positive wording when offering suggestions.

Your conference will also be more successful if you approach the teacher in the proper spirit, trying not to criticize, give advice or express your judgment of the teacher, positive or negative. In other words, simply pick the teacher's brain — ask and listen — and say little.

At the conference, be prepared to hear some negative things about your child and maybe about yourself. Defending your child probably will not help and can cause the conference to deteriorate into an argument. If you will accept responsibility for part of the problem, if there is one, you will open the door for the teacher to consider change, too. You can always reject the teacher's viewpoint *later*, but do not debate it *during* the conference. Take a few days to think it over. After all, the teacher may be correct.

A final key to preparing for a successful conference is having a realistic expectations. Do not expect overnight results from either the teacher or your child. It is hard enough for a principal to change a first-year teacher, much less a teacher who has taught for 20 years! Unfortunately, few interventions at home or school remake a child (Nemko).

A question parents often ask is whether or not their child should participate in a parent/teacher conference and whether one or both parents should participate. Kindergarten and high school students can benefit from participation. The child can better understand the problems and contribute information and profit from observing adults solving a problem. Also, the teacher can observe the relationship between the child and the parent, and the parent can observe how the teacher and student interact.

If you decide to take your child to the conference, the child must understand that 1] the problem is *his* or *hers*, not the teacher's, 2] the child can criticize neither the teacher nor the parent, and 3] the child can give their view of the problem and propose a solution but, as a rule, should listen much and say little (Nemko).

Your child *must* agree to these rules ahead of time. If the child does not agree to these stipulations, leave the child at home. The last thing you need is for the child to "butt" heads with the teacher and/or parents!

It is always a good idea to have both parents attend the conference, but I know that is not always possible. But if one parent cannot attend, maybe a close relative or friend who is genuinely interested can accompany the other parent. Two sets of ears are always better than one, and an extra person can help mend ruffled feathers, keep the conference on a positive course and keep everyone focused on the problem at hand.

After the conference, write the teacher a brief thank-you

note, even if you disagreed with what the teacher said. In addition to showing courtesy, it can remind the teacher to do his or her part, and it can diffuse any negative feelings the conference may have generated.

Sometimes parents leave even successful conferences disappointed, because they came in hoping the teacher could magically solve the problem. But teachers are not magicians. They can only offer suggestions and solutions. The rest is up to you and your child.

Choosing Another Teacher

If your efforts have been unsuccessful, you may want to see the counselor, school psychologist or principal. If after note-writing and a face-to-face conference, you believe that the teacher is the problem, you may want to consider transferring your child to another classroom. Make sure that the new teacher is worth the transfer.

First of all, make sure that transferring your child will solve the problem. Transferring the child out of one classroom into another may be no more than running away from the problem. Further, you may be making your child feel that he/she cannot cope with his/her problems. The timing of such a move is critical. Moves may be more successful early in the school year or the first part of the second semester. They are often easier after a long vacation such as Christmas break. A transfer will require the child to adapt to a new teacher, new routines, new students and new rules. Make sure your child will be able to handle this new situation and that he or she wants this transfer. If the problem does not improve after this rather drastic move, the child's self-esteem can suffer (see Chapter 2, "Self-Esteem and Social Development").

If possible, try to make coping with a poor teacher a learning experience. Since your child will encounter difficult people in his or her life, learning to deal with a poor teacher may be of value in the long run. Remember, too, your child will not always have the "perfect" classroom teacher each year. Some years will be better than others, and, unfortunately, some years will be pretty pathetic.

You can help your child make the best of a poor teacher by asking him/her to think of the teacher as a human being with human failings. Loving the teacher may be impossible but tolerance is not (Nemko).

As a former teacher, I found myself and other teachers working as hard as we could to help both students who helped themselves and concerned parents who were willing to do their part. Thus, writing a note to the teacher and showing your concern may help solve any problems that your child is experiencing. Remember, your child's teacher is a professional educator who sees your child more objectively than you do. Changing teachers and confronting teachers are not ways of finding a solution. Reasonable accommodations by the teacher and solutions to the problem can be found only by keeping the lines of communication open.

In a Nutshell . . .

—   Make sure you understand why a particular test is given, what it measures, and what the results are in relation to your child.
—   Make sure a battery of tests are used rather than a single test to make appropriate recommendations for your child.
—   Psychoeducational evaluations should include not only the disability but your child's strengths as well.

- Keep every report, letter received or written, report cards, mid-semester reports, and anything else that you receive from the school concerning your child.
- Keep files arranged according to school year.
- Use a spiral notebook to record all phone conversations.
- Do not wait for a major problem to develop to contact your child's teacher; take the first step by writing a note.
- When working with the teacher, state the problem as the child's problem and not the teacher's.
- At a parent/teacher conference be prepared to hear negative things about your child and maybe yourself.
- Do not expect overnight results from a parent/teacher conference!
- Keep the lines of communication open.

Frequently Asked Questions Concerning Testing, Record Keeping and Parent/Teacher Conferences

Can't our family physician diagnose LD rather than going through the lengthy and expensive psychoeducational evaluation?

Instead of using just one test or a visit to the family doctor, it is far more effective to determine a disability through several tests and to allow several professionals to form a consensus. A medical doctor is not necessarily schooled to detect LD. With a psychoeducational evaluation, neither one test nor one person makes the final evaluation, which to me is far better than having the opinion of just one person who may or may not be a specialist in LD.

What is aptitude?

Aptitude is the natural ability, capacity or talent in a particular area. For instance, your child may be a brain when it comes to math but may be slow in language. Or your child may be a fine musician.

What do achievement tests reveal?

Achievement tests are designed to assess what a student has learned in relation to other students of the same age and grade level. The tests measure specific types of achievement in academic fields, such as math, reading, language, social studies and science.

Are informational processing and intellectual processing the same thing?

Yes. Both measure how effectively students process, retain and express information they receive through their physical senses, such as hearing, seeing and tasting.

What is the differences between a physical therapist (PT) and an occupational therapist (OT)?

Basically, a physical therapist will test for gross motor skills, muscle tone and balance, whereas an occupational therapist will test for fine motor skills.

Do I have to keep track of every phone call made to the teacher and every piece of paper that my child brings home?

You don't *have* to do anything. However, by tracking each phone call or written notice you may save time and money later. It is quite easy to keep track of these times by simply starting each school year with a new binder with pockets. You can separate each pocket into categories, such as phone calls, parent/teacher conferences, class projects, various classes or any other common threads. As you attend a conference, place your notes in the pocket or, as your child brings notes home, place them in the appropriate pocket. Presto! You are organized! It really is a good habit to get into, and, once organized, it is easy to keep up.

Is it wise to change teachers during the school year, or should you just wait it out?

This really depends on how strongly you and your child feel that the situation warrants such a drastic act. I use the word drastic because changing teachers should be done only as a last resort. Whether your child is LD or not, there will be years that your child may have a teacher whom you and/or your child may not like, get along with or just have bad vibes about. And, too, sometimes the best teachers are not the ones best liked. However, make sure that before you change teachers, the outcome will far outweigh staying with the teacher you have.

See also "Suggested Reading" for Chapter 5, pp. 273-74.

Chapter 6

ADD and ADHD

Understanding the Numbers

The leading psychiatric diagnosis of American children today is hyperactivity. It is the "fashionable" disability for the '90s, and it is estimated that more than 2 million children (or 3 to 5 percent of all children) have the disorder (Hancock 51). The National Institute of Mental Health (NIMH), estimates that about one student in every classroom experiences hyperactivity.

As was previously noted in Chapter 1, between 10 and 20 percent of all school-aged children have learning disabilities and, of those with LD, about 20 to 25 percent will also have Attention Deficit Disorder (ADD) or Attention Deficit Hyperactivity Disorder (ADHD) (Silver 1). Approximately 75 percent of those afflicted with ADD/ADHD will be boys. However, it must be pointed out that LD, ADD and ADHD are separate but related disabilities. Treatment for ADD/ADHD will not correct any LD; they must each be treated separately.

Understanding the History of ADD/ADHD

Over the years, different names have been used to describe hyperactivity, but the term ADD has been used since 1980 to emphasize the attention problem, not hyperactivity, since a deficit in a child's attention seemed to be the major issue. However, to reflect the hyperactivity, the term ADHD was added in 1987. Both terms, ADD/ADHD, are used today, and both are a disability that interferes with a person's ability to sustain attention or focus on a task.

Both ADD/ADHD are characterized by impulsiveness, wandering attention and hyperactivity. If the child is not hyperactive, the diagnosis is ADD. The disorder is most prevalent in children and is generally thought of as a childhood disorder. Recent studies, however, show that ADD/ADHD can continue throughout the adult years. Current estimates suggest that approximately to 50-65 percent of the children with ADD/ADHD will have symptoms of the disorder as adolescents and adults (Barkley).

Scientists and medical experts do not know precisely what causes ADD/ADHD. Scientific evidence suggests that the disorder is genetically transmitted in many cases and is caused by a chemical imbalance or deficiency in certain neurotransmitters (chemicals that regulate the efficiency with which the brain controls behavior). In spring of 1996, scientists found a gene that is linked to excitability in people and suspect this gene may be linked to ADHD. The researchers concluded that the gene probably would not bring on ADHD by itself but, in combination with other genetic or non-genetic factors, could lead to the disorder. No gene for the disorder has been firmly identified, and experts stressed that the finding in the recent study is still preliminary. Today, there is a plethora of active research being conducted on this topic including genetic, physiological and even environmental studies. Scientists do know that ADD and ADHD are *not* the results of brain damage, wrong diet or bad parenting, as some previously surmised.

Suspecting ADD/ADHD

As previously stated, the three main distinctive signals of both ADD and ADHD are inattention, impulsivity and hyperactivity. All children, from time to time, will be inattentive, impulsive and hyperactive, but the child with ADD or ADHD displays these behaviors as the norm and not the exception. If these behaviors are *chronic* and *pervasive* in your child, ADD or ADHD could be the cause. Chronic means that the behaviors have been evident throughout the child's life, and pervasive means that the behaviors are present throughout the child's day.

Because maintaining attention is a skill that can be applied or directed in a variety of ways, the inattentiveness of a child with ADD can take several forms. The child may have difficulty with selective attention such as:

— figuring out where his or her attention needs to be
— focusing attention when he or she knows where attention needs to be but has difficulty zeroing in on the relevant task
— sustaining attention, which is difficulty in maintaining attention in the presence of distractions

—   dividing attention, which is difficulty doing two or more tasks at the same time (Fowler)

The inattentive child is usually described as having a short attention span and being easily distracted because the child is unable to focus on a specific task for a long period of time. The child may have trouble finishing tasks, work, chores or even meals. Problems with listening when directly spoken to and not following directions or instructions are also descriptive of a child with ADD or ADHD. The child with ADD/ADHD gives no attention to details and often makes careless mistakes in schoolwork, work and other activities. Because organizational skills are so poor, the child with ADD/ADHD loses things (toys, keys, school assignments, pencils, pens, books or tools) more readily and is more forgetful. The child with ADD/ADHD can exhibit one or all of these signs.

The dictionary defines *impulsivity* as "acting on impulse," which is a perfect definition of the child with ADHD. These children act first and think later, doing whatever happens to come to mind without regard for the consequences. Impulsive acts can range from trivial to extremely dangerous. These children blurt out answers before questions have been completed, cannot wait their turn and interrupt conversations or games. Because they do not stop to think before they act, they often say something offensive. Usually, they do not realize their error until it is pointed out to them, but sometimes they are sorry they have said something before they even finish saying it.

Children with ADD/ADHD do not learn from experience, because they cannot pause long enough to reflect before they act. They can lose emotional control quite easily and then have great difficulty regaining it. At home, the child may rush through one assignment after another without finishing any. In class, the child will frequently call out answers before the questions have been asked or may attempt to correctly answer a question without raising a hand to speak. Other times, the child will blurt out things intended to be funny. Consequently, these actions cause problems at school, at home and with friends.

Impulsivity can also seriously impair the social interactions of the child (See Chapter 2, "Self-Esteem and Social Development"). These children seem to have a short fuse and get angry easily. Yelling, hitting and throwing become a routine for the child with ADD/ADHD. Their immediate demand to be the first in line, or their tendency to grab things, can be constant sources of irritation to other children.

Hyperactivity may take two forms. First, it can be caused by a particular situation (called *situational* hyperactivity) and may go away either when the situation changes or when the child learns to control the situation. However, the other type of hyperactivity, caused by neurological differences, is called ADHD.

The hyperactive child may not "climb the walls," but they are in constant motion and appear to be restless and fidgety. Even while watching television or playing a game, hyperactive children will be moving some part of their body, ranging from tapping their fingers to squirming in their seat to wiggling their toes. The child runs and climbs excessively, has difficulty sitting still and engages in physical activity not related to the task, such as frequent pencil sharpening or falling out of a chair. The hyperactive child frequently talks loudly and excessively, often without purpose or focus.

One of the hallmarks of this disorder is the pervasiveness of displayed behaviors. If a child only displays these characteristics in one setting, such as at school or at home, then it can probably be attributed to causes other than ADD/ADHD. A child classified as ADD or ADHD will display one or all three behaviors in a chronic and pervasive manner.

The child with ADD/ADHD is often described as immature and lacking in self-awareness, sensitivity and emotional control. The demand for attention is fairly constant; the child is extremely competitive and has a difficult time sharing. They may experience difficulty expressing feelings and accepting responsibility for behavior. The child may get into frequent fights, both verbally and physically. This child often reacts to a social situation without first determining what behavior is desirable. Many times, the child knows what is expected but does not think of the consequences of acting out and acting foolish. Though this child has social problems, it is important to understand that the social skills deficits stem from the disorder. The child definitely wants to have friends, keep friends and wants desperately to be liked and accepted, but, unfortunately, he or she attempts these with inappropriate style.

As a result of these social difficulties, the child either winds up isolated or frequently plays with younger children. The cause for the isolation is obvious and they choose younger children for several reasons. First of all, the maturity level is usually several years lower than the actual chronological age. Secondly, although the maturity level will be on the same level as the younger child, the child with ADD/ADHD will be physically larger so the child with ADD/ADHD tends to be the boss – which suits him or her perfectly.

It is not a bad idea for a child with ADD or ADHD to play with younger children. This is certainly better than having no one at all to play with, but the real acid test of social skills comes in their ability to get along with same age, same sex children.

Understanding the Diagnosis of ADD/ADHD

There is a big difference between suspecting your child has ADD/ADHD and knowing for certain. Parents are cautioned against diagnosing this disorder by themselves. ADD/ADHD is a disability that, without proper identification and treatment, can have serious and long-term complications.

An accurate diagnostic evaluation conducted by a team of well-trained professionals knowledgeable in ADD/ADHD is very important. The ideal professional would be a developmental pediatrician, child psychologist, child psychiatrist or pediatric neurologist.

Diagnosis has remained more of an art form than an exact science, with diagnostic guidelines changing frequently over the years. Typically, the family physician or pediatrician will interview the parents and teachers and take a complete history of the child's behavioral problems in order to rule out other diseases. Your family doctor will ask many questions. Dr. Edward Hallowell, a child psychiatrist (who's also ADHD and LD) and coauthor of *Driven to Distraction* (Simon & Schuster) asks, "How does he get dressed in the morning? How does he behave at dinner, in a restaurant and with other kids?"

A child psychiatrist or other mental health professional may also evaluate your child to assess his or her level of psychological and social functioning and to uncover any emotional conflicts or stresses. An EEG (brain-wave test) or a MRI (an X-ray that gives a picture of the brain's anatomy) are not usually done unless there is a suggestion of a seizure disorder.

Ideally, the full team should meet to discuss what they have found and to establish a diagnosis and treatment plan. The professionals will base their decision, in part, upon on the following behaviors (called criteria) as listed in the American Psychiatric Association's (APA) *Diagnostic and*

Diagnostic Criteria for ADD/ADHD
Diagnostic and Statistical Manual of Mental Disorders (DSM-IV)
(American Psychiatric Association, 1994)

Behaviors must have been present for at least six months, must have begun before the age of seven, and must be present throughout the day. If the child exhibits six or more symptoms of inattention, the child is diagnosed as having ADD. If the child exhibits six or more symptoms of hyperactivity-impulsivity, the diagnosis is ADHD.

Inattention

- often fails to give close attention to details or makes careless mistakes in schoolwork, chores or other activities
- often has difficulty sustaining attention in tasks or play activities
- often does not seem to listen when spoken to directly
- often does not follow through on instructions and fails to finish schoolwork, chores or other duties
- often has difficulty organizing tasks and activities often avoids, dislikes or is reluctant to engage in tasks that require sustained mental effort (such as schoolwork or homework)
- often loses things necessary for tasks or activities (e.g. toys, school assignments, pencils, books or tools)
- is often easily distracted by extraneous stimuli
- is often forgetful in daily activities

Hyperactivity

- often fidgets with hands or feet or squirms in seat (in adolescents, may be limited to subjective feelings of restlessness)
- has difficulty remaining seated when required to do so
- often runs about or climbs excessively in situations in which it is inappropriate
- often has difficulty playing or engaging in leisure activities quietly
- is often "on the go" or often acts as if "driven by a motor", often talks excessively

Impulsivity

- has difficulty awaiting turn in games or group situations
- often blurts out answers to questions before they have been completed
- often interrupts or intrudes on others (e.g., butts into conversations or games)

Statistical Manual of Mental Disorders (DSM-IV) 1994. (see the facing page)

There is no cure or "quick fix" when treating ADD/ADHD. Widely publicized "cures" such as special diets have, for the most part, proven ineffective. Effective treatment of ADD and ADHD generally requires these basic components: education about the disorder, training in the use of behavior management, an appropriate educational program and medication when indicated.

Learning More About ADD/ADHD

Education is key to understanding ADD and ADHD. All professionals who come in contact with children with ADD/ADHD – teachers, mental health professionals and pediatricians – must have a good working knowledge of the facts about basic symptoms, developmental course, causes, diagnosis and treatment. Siblings, grandparents, aunts and uncles, cousins, friends and baby sitters should also learn more about this disorder if they have regular contact with the child. And, of course, most importantly, parents need to become their own "expert" in ADD/ADHD and need to be aware of the symptoms and how those symptoms impact their child's ability to function at home, at school and at social situations.

Children with ADD/ADHD should also be given information (in language and concepts appropriate to their age) about the disorder. Once everyone is on the same wave length and understands that the child cannot help many of his or her problematic behaviors, they will be able to structure situations to enable to the child to behave appropriately and achieve success. Remember, the child who had difficulty with attention, control of impulses and regulating physical activity needs help and encouragement, not agitation, to overcome these problems.

Helping Children With ADD/ADHD

Children with ADD/ADHD respond well to structure. They do best in an organized environment where rules and expectations are clear and consistent, and when consequences for meeting the demands of a given situation are set forth ahead of time and delivered immediately. Thus, the child's environment needs to be organized and predictable. Frequent, consistent praise and rewards for appropriate behavior such as completing tasks on time or being polite and courteous encourage the child to repeat such desirable behavior.

Whether or not children diagnosed as having ADD/ADHD should be classified as students with special educational needs and receive special education services has been a fiercely debated controversy. However, in recent years several events have occurred which will directly and indirectly assist you in communicating and working with your child's school.

The U.S. Department of Education issued a memorandum on September 16, 1991, to all state and local educational agencies which clarified that fact that children with ADD/ADHD may be eligible for support services through the school under the Individuals with Disabilities Education Act of 1990 (IDEA) or Section 504 of the Rehabilitation Act of 1973. (See Chapter 3, "The Law Is On Your Side")

Several well-written resource manuals for teachers were made available which provide a compilation of school interventions for children with ADD (e.g. the *C.H.A.D.D. Educator's Manual*). More teachers are aware of ADD and ADHD and the needs of the children with the disorder in their classrooms, especially due to inclusion (See Chapter 1, "Identification, Diagnosis and Acceptance"). Educators have a greater awareness that effective home-school partnerships are necessary to ensure that students are successful within school.

Understanding the Laws Regarding ADD/ADHD

Children with ADD/ADHD found eligible for services and/or programs through IDEA are most frequently served under the categories of "other health impaired", "learning disabilities" or "serious emotional disturbance". Even when children with ADD/ADHD do not qualify for services through IDEA, they may still be eligible for services through Section 504, which applies to a wider variety of individuals with handicapping conditions. A child with ADD/ADHD would be eligible for school adaptations and interventions under Section 504 if it is determined that ADD/ADHD substantially interfered with a "major life activity," such as learning. If a child with ADD/ADHD comes under IDEA, an IEP (See Chapter 3, "The Law Is On Your Side") will be written that will delineate the difficulties the child is experiencing in school and the steps which will be taken to address those difficulties. Or if the child qualifies under Section 504, an Accommodation Plan will be developed and will provide similar information.

Helping Children With ADD/ADHD in Class

Children with ADD/ADHD are probably as smart or smarter than their peers. But whatever their IQ, children with ADD/ADHD need to have an appropriate educational plan agreed to by the teacher, the parents and the child, if old enough. The poor performance and academic failure of the child with ADD/ADHD usually results from uncompleted tasks, assignments completed in an untimely fashion, disorganization and failure to follow directions.

Children with ADD/ADHD need to sit in front of the classroom to keep focused on the teacher. They will usually need extra time or help with work, such as having someone read tests to them or help with organizing their work. A classroom where activities are highly structured and where the teacher uses a lot of motivation and hands-on instruction is similarly helpful to these children.

Other clever strategies to help these children get through their day include placing masking tape in the hallways so they will be reminded where they should stand; dividing desk tops into different colored segments: one side for work, the other for storage; giving rewards for self-control, appropriate behavior and for other finished tasks; and giving one direction at a time. Additional strategies for use inside and outside the classroom to use with children with ADD/ADHD are listed on the facing and following pages.

Maintaining a good and consistent relationship with your child's teacher is very important, especially if your child is having trouble. It is very hard for a parent to discuss serious and emotionally loaded issues with strangers. Therefore, if your child is going into a new class with a new teacher, and the child is encountering considerable problems, try to arrange a meeting *before* the school year begins. Continue to maintain parent/teacher contact throughout the year. Working with the school system and the teacher will help your child gain success not only socially but also academically.

Someone once said that if you maliciously set out to produce an environment that could daily drive an ADD/ADHD child crazy, you could not come up with anything worse than school. How right they are. School requires that children not

Accommodations for Children With ADD/ADHD

Children with ADD/ADHD often times have many serious problems in school. Whether they are academic or social, problems seem to follow the child with ADD/ADHD. If you are lucky enough to have your child in a classroom with a teacher who is sensitive to the problems of ADD and ADHD, consider yourself *extremely* fortunate. However, that may not be the case, but there are some tried-and-true tactics which teachers can employ without going to great lengths to modify their teaching or their classroom. It is quite easy for you to recommend these techniques to teachers without offending them. Simply suggest, "At home we use . . ." or "My husband and I do this . . ." Explaining to the teacher what works at home can allow the teacher to incorporate successful strategies into the classroom quite easily. Picture how the following accommodations could help your child and notice how simple each of these accommodations is. If even one of the following will help alleviate the stress at home or at school, it will be worth a phone call to the teacher or a visit to the school.

Inattention

- seat the child near a role model
- increase the distance between desks
- break long assignments into smaller parts so a child can see an end to the assignment
- give assignments one at a time to avoid work overload
- give clear, concise instructions
- have a secret code between child and teacher to remind child to stay on task

Impulsiveness

- ignore minor inappropriate behavior
- increase immediacy of rewards and consequences
- use time-out procedure for misbehavior
- acknowledge positive behavior of nearby student
- set up a behavior contract

continued on the next page

Accommodations for Children With ADD/ADHD *continued*

Socialization

- praise appropriate behavior
- set up social behavior goals with child and implement a reward program
- provide small group social skills training
- praise child frequently
- prompt appropriate social behavior either verbally or with private signal
- set up a behavior contract

Compliance

- instruct child in self-monitoring of behavior
- use contracts
- seat student near teacher
- use teacher attention to reinforce positive behavior
- provide immediate feedback

Moodiness

- provide reassurance and encouragement
- speak softly in nonthreatening manner if child shows nervousness
- send positive notes home
- make time to talk alone with student
- reinforce frequently when signs of frustration are noticed

Academic Skills

- provide additional reading time if reading is weak
- avoid oral reading
- shorten amount of required reading
- if oral expression is weak – accept all reasonable oral responses
- encourage talking about new ideas or experiences
- pick topics easy for child to talk about
- if written language is weak– accept non-written forms for reports
- encourage the use of a computer
- accept use of typewriter and tape recorder

continued on the next page

Accommodations for Children With ADD/ADHD *continued*

- do not assign large quantity of written work
- encourage use of books on tape
- test with multiple choice or fill in the blanks
- if math is weak– use graph paper to space numbers
- provide additional math time
- provide immediate correctiveness feedback and instruction via modeling of the correct computational procedure
- use a calculator
- encourage after-school tutoring

Organizational Skills

- encourage use of notebook with dividers and folders for work
- send daily/weekly progress reports home
- give assignments one at a time
- allow child a second set of books for home
- regularly check desk and notebook for neatness
- encourage neatness rather than penalize sloppiness

---

only sit still, but also concentrate on material. Sitting still and concentration are two words that are not part of their vocabulary.

Difficulty with rules and self-restraint often make the child with ADD/ADHD a significant negative force in the classroom. The child often gets into a vicious circle with the teacher: the child acts up; the teacher tries to control the child; the child resists by acting up more; the teacher exerts more control, and on and on. By April, the teacher has had it, and so has the child.

Medicating Children Who Have ADD/ADHD

Medication has proven effective for many children with ADD/ADHD. Doctors have long used Ritalin, a common stimulant, to treat children with ADD and ADHD. Like an amphetamine, Ritalin produces in normal individuals a feeling of euphoria in large doses, but it can also cause sleeplessness, weight loss, irritability, nausea, dizziness and headaches. For reasons not fully understood, it also helps control impulsiveness in many ADD/ADHD children and adults.

The stimulant drugs (Ritalin and other, similar drugs used to treat ADD/ADHD) can be a godsend for those who truly need it. "Ritalin is one of the raving successes in psychiatry," says Dr. Lawrence Greenhill of Columbia University Medical School. Now it is a routinely prescribed drug at distinguished institutions from Johns Hopkins to the Mayo Clinic. It is a medication that allows children and a growing number of adults to focus their minds and rein in their rampaging attention spans.

How does this drug work? Researchers believe that Ritalin speeds up the central nervous system. The drug appears to have its own attention deficit, taking effect in 30 minutes and then losing effectiveness after three or four hours. Children usually take 5 to 10 milligrams (mg) three times a day for prime-time schoolwork. While some parents allow their children with ADD/ADHD to take "drug holidays," such as on weekends (*Newsweek*), other parents have told me they believe this practice is akin to taking a child's prescription eye glasses away from them.

Before randomly taking your child off Ritalin (or other drugs used to treat ADD/ADHD) for any amount of time, check first with your child's prescribing physician to learn about problems which might occur if your child is on a "drug holiday". For example, if your child has an afternoon or weekend job, he or she might need to continually take his or her medication to be able to focus attention to responsibilities at work. The same holds true for driving-aged ADD/ADHD children, who need to be able to pay attention while behind the wheel. Be careful and cautious about dropping ADD/ADHD medication for even a day.

An estimated 1.5 million children in the United States between the ages 5 and 18 are believed to be taking Ritalin, according to a recent study by Dr. Daniel Safer of Johns Hopkins University's School of Medicine. One survey of physicians places that figure even higher, at 2.6 million users nationwide. That translates into about one child in every classroom, or 3 to 5 percent of the entire school-age population.

Although Ritalin is the number-one choice of stimulants prescribed by physicians for controlling impulsiveness and inattention, there are two other stimulants that can also be used with success in treating ADD and ADHD. Dexedrine and Cylert both carry the same side effects as Ritalin, but the costs between the three are quite different. Ritalin (a brand name) has a generic name (methylphenidate) and runs from $30 to $45 per 100 at 15 milligrams (mg). Dexedrine and Cylert, for the same amount and dosage, are approximately $75 and $125, respectively. Antidepressants have also been used to decrease hyperactivity and aggression. Tofranil, Norpramin and Elavil are three such antidepressants. Side effects from them include dizziness, drowsiness, weight gain and fatigue.

Understanding the Ritalin Controversy

Even with other stimulants and antidepressants to choose from, doctors still prescribe Ritalin much more often than the other choices. Ritalin is classified by the U.S. Drug Enforcement Administration (DEA) as a Schedule II controlled substance in the same category as cocaine, methadone and methamphetamine. Thus, dependency can eventually become a problem. This is another reason not to abruptly stop administration of Ritalin or other stimulant-type drugs.

And believe it or not, "Vitamin R," one of Ritalin's recreational names, has become an abused drug on the playground, which is good reason for parents to keep tight control of their children's medications. Since most school districts have adopted a policy that does not allow children to come to school carrying medications (even aspirin), parents should not give children their medication to take "on their own" while at school. If ADD/ADHD medication needs to be administered while the child is at school, parents should arrange for school officials to administer it.

On the street, Ritalin sells for $3 to $15 per pill to be crushed and snorted for a cheap and relatively modest buzz. The DEA warns that the "smart drug" may become a problem "street drug" in the near future. Aside from one death due to Ritalin overdose in April, 1996, the numbers of abusers seem to be relatively small. Scientists believe Ritalin will have a tough time making an appearance on the favorite-party-drug list because it is too complex to manufacture illegally, and it does not create a euphoria similar to that of cocaine.

Despite the controversy over Ritalin and its side effects, life today may be a lot easier with it. Many generations of people with ADD and ADHD have spent miserable childhoods failing at school and friendships and watching their stressed families struggle. Out of frustration, many of these children act out and wind up in the criminal justice system. To researchers, it is a classic "pay now or pay more later" situation. NIMH studies indicate that those with untreated ADD and ADHD are more likely to become alcoholics, smokers or drug abusers then the general population. More than 33 percent drop out of school, says Russell Barkley, Director of Psychology at the Worcester Medical Center of the University of Massachusetts, and about ten percent of ADHD adults attempt suicide.

According to the NIMH, Ritalin is a positive treatment for 90 percent of the ADD/ADHD children who require medication. Yet, experts believe that Ritalin is not a cure-all for ADD/ADHD but rather just one aspect of an effective treatment plan.

Finding Help Outside of the Pharmacy

Parents, doctors and teachers agree that children with ADD/ADHD need additional work on behavior, since hyperactivity is its own issue and not always affected by Ritalin. A combination of the following is a more comprehensive approach than medication alone:

— positive parenting
— discipline
— a daily, weekly, and monthly reward system to encourage appropriate behavior (behavior modification in an educational plan to which you, the child and the teacher can agree.)
— the use of medication (if necessary)

Working together, these efforts will help the child with ADD/ADHD compensate their disability.

Identifying LD in the Child With ADD/ADHD

One last diagnostic problem should be mentioned: the difficulty discriminating ADD/ADHD from LD. There are several ways of attempting to discriminate one from the other. The first is the developmental history. At age two or three most LD-only children will *not* show symptoms such as hyperactivity and impulsivity. Next, LD can sometimes be ruled out if there is *no* gap between IQ and achievement, assuming other measures have also been considered (see Chapter 5, "Testing, Record Keeping and Parent/Teacher Conferences"). Further, consistent comments about distractibility and short attention spans, throughout the early school years, indicate ADD/ADHD. Finally, a medication trial can often eliminate many ADD/ADHD symptoms. If the medicated child appears normal and shows no academic handicaps or underachievement, it would appear that the problem is ADD/ADHD alone. Experts generally agree that medication will not remediate a true learning disability (Phelan 69).

This chapter covers only the bare essentials of this disorder. If you suspect, or if your child has been diagnosed with ADD/ADHD, it is imperative that you gather, read and understand how this disorder is diagnosed, the reasonable approaches that can be employed at home, and methods of effective interaction with school personnel. Use your local library and the Internet to keep current on issues related this disorder. Being well informed will empower you to make sensible decisions about your child with ADD/ADHD.

In a Nutshell . . .

- ADD and ADHD are often lifelong disorders.
- Medication is only one method for treating this disorder.
- LD and ADD and ADHD are related disorders, but they are not the same; each must be diagnosed and separately treated.
- Ritalin has proven to be an effective medication for controlling impulsiveness and inattention.
- A system of positive parenting, behavior modification, effective educational planning and medication, if necessary, will help the child with ADD/ADHD compensate for this disability.

Frequently Asked Questions Concerning ADD and ADHD

Are all children with ADD hyperactive?

No. Many people seem to associate hyperactivity with attention deficits, but it is only one part of the equation. Many children have a hard time concentrating on a task, and are impulsive, yet they are not hyperactive.

What do I do if I think my child has ADD/ADHD?

If you think your child has ADD, schedule a medical evaluation through the school system, a developmental pediatrician, a child psychologist, a child psychiatrist or a pediatric neurologist. Make sure whoever does the testing uses a multidisciplinary evaluation. If you are near a university-based hospital, ask your pediatrician for referral if that university does this type of testing. Going through the university system may even cost you less.

Is medication effective in treating ADD?

Experts say that 90 percent of children with ADD/ADHD benefit from medication. But medication is only part of the solution. Behavior management, family counseling, and an educational plan also need a also be used with the medication.

Are there support groups available for parents?

There are a few groups for parents of children with ADD. One more popular group is C.H.A.D.D., which provides parents with support and information about children with ADD. Their address is 1859 North Pine Island Road, Suite 185, Plantation, FL 33322, phone (305) 384-6869.

Are children with ADD/ADHD classified as special education students?

Under recent legislation IDEA, children with ADD can receive special education services if their diagnoses fall within one of three classifications. ADD itself is not a specific special education category.

Does sugar make children with ADD hyperactive?

No proof exists that the level of sugar causes ADD.

Should children with ADD/ADHD be in a special education classroom?

Most children with ADD are in a regular classroom and may receive special educational services depending upon their specific need. ADD/ADHD does not mean they need to be in a special class.

Will insurance cover ADD/ADHD treatment?

Every insurance company is different but unfortunately, most do not or are reluctant to provide coverage, citing reasons such as preexisting condition rules or claiming that ADD is not a medical diagnosis. However, there are two current areas need your attention. First, Congress is getting more and more involved with health insurance issues. Keep in touch with your elected officials and make your case known to them. Secondly, because ADD is finally being recognized in adults, insurance companies may take a second look at this disorder.

Can you have all three: LD, ADD and ADHD?

Yes and no. Approximately 25 to 30 percent of children with LD are diagnosed with ADD or ADHD. ADD refers only to attention and not hyperactivity; therefore, if your child is diagnosed with ADHD, he or she has a deficit in attention and he or she has hyperactivity. If your child has a deficit in only attention, then the diagnosis is ADD.

See also "Suggested Reading" for Chapter 6, pp. 274-75.

School Options

Choosing the right school for your child – a school that is not only knowledgeable about LD but willing to accommodate your child's LD – can be one of the most frustrating adventures a parent can face. But do not give up. There is help available if you know what to ask and where to go. Read on!

The next three chapters discuss various school options for children with LD which will help you decide which option would best fit your child's learning style and disability. I have included in the appendices a cost analysis worksheet to be used to determine how much each educational option will cost. However, in making your final decision base your decision on all factors and not just cost. When reading each chapter, keep in mind that spending thousands of dollars on professionals and schools will not guarantee that your child will be successful or that the LD problem will disappear. You must dig much deeper than your wallet to find the school that best fits your child. Remember, there is no such thing as a *perfect* school, only one that best fits your child's learning style and personality.

Chapter 7

School Option #1: Public Schools

The Constitution of the United States does not guarantee each of us an education, but it does give Congress the power to provide for the "general welfare of the United States." Congress has used this power as a basis for educational matters which affect Americans, such as the passage of PL 94-142 and IDEA (See Chapter 3, "The Law Is On Your Side"). But the real catalyst for education came with the passage of the Northwest Ordinance in 1787, which, among other things, stated that "means of education shall forever be encouraged." For example, as towns and villages developed, a plot of land in the center of each town was set aside for education. That same idea, born in 1787, is still alive and well.

Today, most counties have several lower, middle and high schools, but parents still send their child to the school that is nearest to their home because school districts are created within the counties. That choice is not always the best school for your child. Upon observing schools, whether near your home or across town, you will find that not all schools are created equal and that public schools, in general, vary from district to district. In fact, as one criteria for buying or renting, many parents choose homes based on the neighborhood schools.

Historically, premier schools were usually located in the more affluent neighborhoods. Today's parents are willing to pay more real estate taxes if they feel they are getting the best schools in exchange. What parents do not know is that, no matter how much they pay in taxes or contribute to a politician's future, there is no guarantee their local school is better than the one across town. Taxes are only one ingredient to having one of the best schools.

Finding the Best Public Schools

Today it is easier than ever to have your child placed in any school in your district. In the late 1980s, school choice became a popular theme in public education. School choice is just what it says – choosing which public school you want your child to attend within the district and, in some cases, changing districts. By the 1990s, school choice had been widely discussed by parents and school officials and finally made its way to the state legislatures to be debated. Soon, states were passing laws which enabled parents to choose which public school their child would attend. No longer would parents be held hostage to their neighborhood's school. This is a far better method than that of being assigned to a school based on one's address.

What everyone found, when parents chose the school

for their child, was a better match of the child's needs with the school's strengths. Parental choice also led to parents playing a more active role in supporting their choice.

So, if you find that your neighborhood school may not be as accommodating as you need it to be and there is a school in your county that you want your child to attend, you should request a transfer through the proper channels. Start by calling the school administration and ask for the procedure. Each school administration has a set of steps to follow. Follow these steps as outlined by the school administration and remember that patience and perseverance go a long way.

Just because a child is LD does not mean he or she cannot be gifted in another area, such as the arts. If you have a gifted child who is also LD but excels in one of the arts, there are public schools in some states which group students together according to their gifted area. These schools are called "magnet" schools and are similar to the preprofessional private schools (See Chapter 8, "School Option #2: Private Day and Boarding Schools") but are even more competitive, with an acceptance rate of less than 20 percent. Because magnet schools teach only to the child's strengths, they do not usually offer LD support, tutoring or therapies, and they probably do not want to deal with any LD problems (but be sure to ask). Magnet schools maintain a very structured environment, and any free time your child might have will be used to increase their skill areas. Magnet schools offer wonderful opportunities for young, talented students, but they are not for everyone. Not all states or counties offer this type of public schooling, but it is certainly worth looking at — if *and only if* your child wants to pursue this option. Do not think for a moment that this is a substitute for the LD problem. Before offering this option to your child, make sure you understand the extent of your child's LD, realizing that by making this choice and not addressing the LD problem now, the child's problems could be magnified later in life.

Finding the right public school education is similar to buying a new car. When looking for a new car you do not just go into any dealership and pick out a car. Instead, you will spend many hours and days, and maybe months, reading ads, "haggling," checking out car dealerships, test driving various cars, interviewing other owners of cars that you are considering, then comparing maybe one to three cars just to see which one fits your needs, the needs of your family and your wallet. For the most part, the average person checks around before buying or ordering a particular car.

The procedure for finding the right school for your child is very similar. You need to visit the school(s), talk to parents, teachers and principal(s), and then compare each component before you arrive at a decision. I am sure that the very thought of visiting the principal makes you shudder, but remember it is your child's future you are discussing. Should you not spend as much time or more on selecting the school for your child as you would selecting a new car? Think about it.

Before commencing on this endeavor of finding the public school that best fits your child's needs, ask other parents, relatives, friends and the professionals who tested your child which schools are the best and which schools have the teachers who are best prepared to work with children with LD. They will be your best source for information on where to begin with your search. Keep in mind, though, that each person will give his or her own opinion, therefore, little consensus will be reached. You will still need to do your own homework.

Prior to the interview, the parent should have a handle on the LD problem — i.e., know as much as you can on the type and extent of your child's LD problem(s). The next question is: do you place your child in a school that offers LD support and/or some LD classes or do you put your child in general education classrooms (inclusion) rather than in a self-contained classroom with a maximum of 15 students and possibly one teacher's aide (special education).

Understanding Inclusion

One of the hotly debated topics in LD education today is *inclusion*. Inclusion, "full inclusion," "full integration," "unified system" and "inclusive education" are terms used to describe a popular policy or practice in which all students with disabilities, regardless of the nature or severity of the disability and need for related services, receive their total education within the regular education classroom. Some parents of children with LD feel that putting their child in a special education class singles the child out from their peers. They feel the school should accommodate children with LD in such a way as to include them in every class.

There is a happy medium between inclusion, which is one extreme, and special education, which is the other extreme. However, the choice you make will depend on the extent of your child's LD and your child's learning style. Some children will do much better being placed in a smaller class, such as special education class, while being mainstreamed into other classes, such as art, physical education and music. On the other hand, your child's LD problem may affect only one or two subject areas, such as math or reading. In that case, your child may not need full-time special education classes. Heavy-duty LD support within the regular classroom may be the best option.

The program you choose will depend upon the extent of the LD problem(s) of your child. In making your decision, take into account what the experts suggest, but if your "gut" decision says something different than what the experts suggest, go with your "gut" decision. Professional opinions cannot take the place of personal instinct. And besides, who knows your child better than you, the parent?

Interviewing the Principal

The principal at any public school makes or breaks the school. He or she sets the tone for academics, the morale of the faculty and the overall character of the school, and he or she is the instructional leader for the school. Therefore, it is most important that you interview the principal. Before visiting a school, make an appointment with the principal. Tell the person setting up the appointment that you need 10 to 15 minutes of the principal's time because you have several questions that you would like to ask and be sure to mention that some of the questions deal with the LD and/or special education programs at the school. If the principal cannot carve out 10 minutes for you, then maybe that is not the best school for your child. However, most principals will be more than happy to meet with you, and if they are secure in what they are doing, they will be happy to answer your questions.

When you meet with the principal, be sure to explain in a candid way why you are there and why you will be asking some direct questions and taking notes. If you do this from the start, the principal will not think you are there as a spy for the local newspaper or from the school board! Put yourself in his or her shoes. You would most likely be a little suspicious if you were being interviewed and did not know why.

The following is a list of questions you should ask the principal before enrolling your child. As you read each question, picture how this question relates to your child's LD and why it is important. These questions are only suggestions, and you will need to ask only the pertinent questions that relate to your child. I would also suggest that you either write down the questions on index cards or make a form to follow. Another suggestion would be to ask first those questions which require only simple answers (yes, no, how many). Follow the simple questions with the more detailed questions. This simply gives the principal time to gather information on the LD program at the school and does not put the principal in a defensive position. Remember, once you make your choice of schools, you will eventually have to work with one of the principals at some point or another, so start out on the right foot and not in an adversarial role.

How many LD teachers and/or special education teachers are there for each grade?

The reason for this question is obvious. Maybe your child reacts better to a male teacher versus a female teacher or to a more permissive teacher rather than a strict teacher. If you have a choice of teachers, you will later have the option of a transfer, should it become necessary. The more teachers at each grade level, the better the chance to find the right match.

How many teacher's aides are assigned full time to LD classes and/or special education classes, if any? How many are assigned to regular classrooms?

This is an important question, since many school districts are eliminating teachers' aides due to funding shortfalls. Make sure you ask if there are full-time aides in individual classes, because many are now being shared between several classes rather than just one per class. Teacher's aides can help make a big class seem smaller and can free the teacher to give extra help to those who need it. Aides also can help give out that extra TLC that all students crave.

Are parents encouraged to volunteer in the classroom(s) or in the school?

Give extra points to this question if parents *are* encouraged to volunteer. Many schools discourage parent participation, but parent involvement has a positive side effect. Even if the school has teacher's aides, involving parents frees up additional precious time that will allow the teacher to spend more time with the students.

What type of school recognition does the school use?

Remember when you were in school and only the smartest, prettiest and brightest received awards? Remember how you envied those kids, wishing you could be just as smart, just as pretty and just as bright? Whether you are 5 years or 50 years old, you want to be recognized. Children should be recognized on an ongoing basis and not just the last day of school and not just for being pretty, smart or athletic. The recognition needs to be school wide and each student should have the opportunity to achieve and be recognized.

What type of formal curriculum does the school have?

This question is most important if you are considering inclusion. If the principal seems vague, you can best assume there is no clear curriculum and each teacher makes up his or her own. The child with LD is better off when teachers make up the curriculum rather than following one dictated by the administration. They can then make up lesson plans which work best for each class. Of course, if your child is scheduled for special education classes, this question is not relevant, since the IEP will dictate the curriculum.

How does the principal feel about students with LD and the LD program at his/her school? Or how does the principal feel about special education classes or program at the school?

Ask the principal if he is familiar with IDEA (1990) and PL 94-142 (1975). If so, ask what he or she thinks of the IEP. This will also tell you if he or she *really* understands the law. Also, check out the principal's facial and vocal expressions. They may tell more than the words used to express the opinion.

Is inclusion part of the LD program at this school, and how does the principal feel about inclusion?

This question is pertinent only if you are interested in inclusion for your child. Parents and older students must decide together which direction they may want to take.

Are there additional professional and support staff, such as speech therapy, occupational therapy (OT) and physical therapy (PT) available on a daily or weekly basis?

Zero in on the particular therapy that your child may need. Your child's IEP will document how frequently your child will receive the service, so make sure the school has the support personnel required in the IEP. Again, because of budget cuts and so many children are in need of support services, these staffs are visiting many more schools. As a result, all schools are served but with much less time allocated for the service.

For the high school student, ask what kind of diploma your child will receive if he or she attends LD classes or is placed in special education classes.

This is a very important question for a high school student and parents because each state may have different rules regulating the type of diploma. For example, in Florida, a child placed in special education classes may receive a restricted diploma. Therefore, when this student tries to gain admission to the state community college, he or she would first have to pass a Graduate Equivalency Degree (GED) test, which is equivalent to a high school diploma. Get what you can in writing from the school district and make sure you understand the full impact of the type of diploma that your child would receive if he or she were in LD or special education classes.

Are classes grouped by student ability or by random selection?

If you are considering inclusion, then this question is most important. Grouping students by ability or random selection has been debated for years with no overwhelming conclusions for either side. Self-esteem usually suffers in mixed classes because, no matter how much work they do or how hard they work, the children with LD will still never fare better than their classmates and perhaps fare much worse. However, students with LD placed in a mixed classes will feel better about themselves because they were not placed in the slower or lower-level class that their classmates might refer to as "the dumb class."

How well does the school do on achievement tests?

Usually, principals are the first to brag about how well their students performed on achievement tests. When you ask the principal this question, notice how he or she reacts. Timed achievement tests hurt the scores of student with LD the most. If you think your child will be low achieving on standardized tests, then you may want your child to attend a school with slightly lower achievement test scores, since your child may have a better chance of maintaining good self-esteem and not blamed for lowering the achievement test scores at the school.

Depending on your child's special needs, you may want to ask what special needs or interests the school may offer.

This would include any before- and after-school activities, sports, music and art classes and any other special interest your child may have. Also, ask if there is a fee for any of the "extras." Today, it is not unusual to find before- and after-school day care available through the public school system as more and more parents enter the work force.

Is there a budget for field trips, and are special education and LD classes part of that budget?

This is a legitimate question, especially if your child learns through seeing or feeling. Because of budget cuts, many schools are allowing only one field trip per class for the entire year. Regardless of the age or grades involved, there should be a budget for field trips. If field trips are not planned in the school budget, ask where extra money can be found for including these in the curriculum. Through fund-raising activities and support from the Parent/Teacher Organization (PTO) and other school and civic groups, money can probably be found.

After your interview, ask if you could visit one or two classrooms. You may want to request a particular teacher(s) whom your child might eventually have. Most principals will allow you to observe classes. However, they will need to contact the teacher ahead of time to make sure that you will not disturb any of the classes' work. Thank the principal for his or her time and always follow up with a thank-you note.

As you walk through the halls to find the class you are to observe, walk slowly, peeking inside a few of the classrooms along the way. Observe quickly what the students and teacher are doing. Is there a one-on-one teaching environment? Are the classes orderly? Do the children seem to be listening? You can take a quick look and know right away what is happening. As you walk the hallways, is student work displayed on the walls? Are the walls cheerful or are they blank? How does the lighting affect the mood of the school? As you pass students and teacher(s) in the hall, is there a friendly greeting? Do the students act orderly in class as well as in the hall? Is the school clean and well maintained? What is the general feeling of the school — friendly, warm and caring or cold, dull and definitely not friendly? If your reception with the principal was warm, chances are the school will be, too. Nothing can make or break a school like a principal.

Observing a Classroom

Your actual classroom observation will last 15 to 20 minutes. Do not overstay your welcome. Here are a few questions that you should be able to answer in your mind during your observation:

— Are the students spending most of their time on worthwhile activities?
— Does the teacher interact with the students?
— Does the teacher use facial expressions? Is most of the work done in a monotone with no inflection or enthusiasm?
— Does the teacher spend any one-on-one, quality time with the students?
— How does the teacher use the teacher's aide?
— How many positive comments do you hear during that brief observation?
— Are parents volunteering in the class, and how is that working out?
— Does the teacher address individual student needs?
— Does the teacher seem to care about the students or is this just a job?
— Finally, and most importantly, are the students learning and do they seem happy to be part of the class you are observing?

Inspecting the Playground, Library and Lunchroom

As you leave the classroom, quietly thank the teacher and try to leave via the playground, library or lunchroom, or, if time permits, visit each of these areas. If you visit at recess time, check to see how the children interact with each other. Do they play as a group, or are there cliques? Do the teachers try to include all students in play, or do they just stand around and talk to one another? What is the condition of the equipment? Is there enough for everyone to find something to do?

As for the library, how many books are available for check out at one time, and how many reference books are available? Are there current periodicals and newspapers? Are the periodicals and reference books age-appropriate for that school? If you can talk to the librarian, find out what the budget is for buying new books each year. Also, learn how many classes can fit into the library at one time? Is the use of the library encouraged?

Finally, visit the lunchroom. Is it clean? Are the students orderly? It takes only a minute to visit the lunchroom, with students or without. The odor and cleanliness will say it all. If you visit during lunch, how are the students behaving? If possible, talk to the head of the lunchroom and ask about special diets, such as low fat, vegetarian offerings, or a salad bar, if these choices would apply to your child.

The entire process of observing the school, interviewing the principal, and observing a classroom should not take more than an hour. When you complete your visit to the first school, write down as many thoughts and observations as you can while they are still fresh in your memory. Take a break and then continue with your next visit. Do not try to do more than three schools in one day. After finishing the target school list, relax and then compare and decide which school would best fit your child's needs.

In a Nutshell . . .

- There is no perfect school for your child, only one that best fits your child's learning style and personality.
- Spending thousands of dollars on professionals and schools is no guarantee that your child will be successful or that the LD problem will disappear.
- The principal sets the tone for academics, for morale of the faculty and for the overall character of the school. To select the best available public school, it is imperative that you interview the principal.
- In making your final decision on a public school, analyze each situation and go with your "gut" decision.

Frequently Asked Questions Concerning Public Schools

What is school choice?

School choice is just what it says — choosing which public school you want your child to attend within the district and, in some cases, changing districts.

Is school choice universal or is it available in only a few states?

As yet, school choice is not universal, but school choice is a popular topic that more and more school boards and school districts are debating. Every state, county and/or school district policy will vary, so check with your local school district. Also, if your school district offers school choice, and you wish for your child to attend a school outside his or her school district, apply as early as possible, since there may be a cutoff in the number who can transfer to the school of choice or even a cutoff in the number of applicants who can apply for a transfer. In other words, get your application in as soon as possible.

How can I have my child attend a public school that is out of our school district?

If your area does not have a school choice, but you want your child to attend a school outside your school district, call your school administration and ask what channels you must go through to get your child enrolled at a certain school. Also, apply for the school transfer as far in advance as possible, since many times those who ask first get their choice.

How do I apply for my child to attend a "magnet" school in my area?

Again, every state, county, school district and/or school board is different. Most of the time, though, students either audition (if it's a performing arts school) or are tested and then asked to attend the magnet schools. If your child excels in an area where a magnet school can accommodate your child's expertise, then apply, but make sure that the school is aware of your child's LD. Also find out in advance if the school intends to accommodate your child's LD. Remember, magnet schools teach only to the child's strength, and that will be good for the self-esteem. However, that does not compensate for the LD.

I am new to a community. How do I find the best school in the area for my child with LD?

First, join a local support group (see the list of national chapters found at the end of Chapter 4) and ask those parents where their child attends and then ask for their opinion on the teachers and the school. That would be your best source. If your area does not have a support group, you can call the state LDA (contact the national LDA office at (412) 341-1515 to get your state's office number), then ask for help through the state office. Chances are, one of their state officers lives in your area, and they can put you in touch with a local support group. Also, another source is to ask neighbors, relatives and business associates who have school-age children. These sources may not be directly involved with the school LD program, but in all probability they do know a family who is and can put you in touch with that family.

What is inclusion?

Inclusion as the name implies, means including all students with disabilities, regardless of the nature or severity of the disability and need for special services, receive their total education within the regular education classroom. Other names associated with inclusion are: full inclusion, full integration, unified system and inclusive education.

For a child with LD, isn't inclusion the best situation, since it would help with self-esteem?

Not necessarily. It would depend upon the degree of the child's disability. Inclusion certainly is good for the child's ego, since it does not single out a child because of his or her disability. If your child's disability is severe, inclusion is probably not the best situation. But if your child has only minor or only a single disability, inclusion with a heavy dose of tutoring may be right for your child. As a parent, it is necessary for you to know the extent of your child's disability for you and your child (if old enough) to decide on what classroom situation is best suited for his or her disability.

Is it absolutely necessary to interview the principal before deciding on a particular school?

There are not too many things in life that are *absolutely* necessary, and interviewing a principal is not one of them. However, if you are going to take the time to observe a classroom, then taking a few more minutes to talk with the principal shouldn't kill you. How better to find out about a school than to talk to the principal? Remember, the principal sets the tone for academics, morale and the character of the school.

See also "Suggested Reading" for Chapter 7, p. 276.

Chapter 8

School Option #2: Private Day and Boarding Schools

Many wonderful private day and boarding schools offer programs specifically geared to the student with LD. Some schools accept only students with LD while others accept a portion who are mainstreamed in the regular academic classes, a tactic similar to inclusion in public education. In addition, children with LD attend LD classes with emphasis on their unique learning disability. However, in evaluating each school, you need to be certain that the school's LD program is one that will meet your child's specific needs and not just give general LD support. Unfortunately, in order to increase the school's enrollment, admission counselors have sometimes accepted students with LD to their school and, at the same time, hired a tutor to help the students with LD. Tutoring is no substitute for an actual LD program. So before you embark on a quest for that perfect private school, know your child's needs so you will be able to see how the different programs will fit into your child's education.

Understanding Private Schools

Various kinds of private schools are available for both the child with LD and the child without it. Besides the basic private day school, there are military, religious and boarding schools. Under those headings comes single-sex or coeducational as well as preprofessional and postgraduate schools. Before seeking that "just right" school for your child, you need to familiarize yourself with the types available.

Military Schools

Military schools have had a reputation, rooted in the 1950s, as a place for the wealthy to send their sons for strict discipline. They were especially popular after World War II, when Americans were feeling proud to be nationalistic. For the American family, sending their child to a military school was something of a status symbol as well as the best way to ensure a good education. In addition, the son was learning to be a great American and a future leader.

However, the military climate in America changed drastically as the war in Vietnam escalated. As a result, military schools became less and less popular. In fact, there was a 10-year period when military school enrollment dropped so drastically that many closed their doors forever. However, with the end of the Vietnam war, military schools soon regained their popularity.

Today's military schools have changed considerably since the 1950s. For the most part, military schools no longer accept problem boys, and they have also cut back on their rigid military training. Additionally, many are now are co-ed. The only substantial difference between military schools and other private schools is the military training and discipline, which is definitely not as strict or rigid as it was during the 1950s.

In deciding whether your child would be interested in a military school, you must decide whether your child will flourish in a setting where military-styled uniforms are required at all times. Strict codes of military discipline and obedience to orders issued by student superior officers, as well as adults, are heeded. Many students who attend military schools think they are fun, but do not consider this alternative if you and your child are not in total agreement with the military "philosophy." This is of particular importance if part of your child's behavior problems include an inability to follow directions.

Religious Schools

Parochial and independent are the two basic types of religious schools. A parochial school is generally owned and operated by the church and clergy and is subject to no outside interference by parents, state authorities or anyone else. An example includes Roman Catholic schools, which are located in every state and most communities across the United States and around the world. Independent religious schools have no direct legal ties to the church or clergy. Like all independent schools, they are operated by a board of trustees or directors, which may or may not include clergy, but the board is usually comprised of members of a common religion whose goal may be the propagation of their beliefs (Unger).

There are many outstanding religious schools, but be wary of them since schools run by clergy may or may not have trained educators and may put teaching the faith ahead of teaching academics or helping the child with LD. Most of these church schools have very limited enrollment and, because of that, you may feel that if your child is placed in a classroom setting with only three to six other children, there will be more individualized education for your child. Unfortunately, this is not always the case. Many church schools get their funding from the church, but if the church has a small congregation, it really cannot properly provide the needed supplies, materials, qualified teachers, equipment and books.

Also, beware of church schools or Christian schools which opened their doors in the 1970s, particularly in the South. Founded solely to avoid desegregation and to skirt federal court orders, such schools not only censor, but often have rewritten vast bodies of knowledge to conform with often backward religious and racial beliefs and prejudices (Unger). If you check with the educational requirements of the teachers who are hired to teach in these schools, you will find that many, if not all, graduated from the same college, majoring in religion and Christian education, and you will find that they really do not have a background for teaching academics.

City Schools

A private school in the city offers many advantages, such as availability of cultural attractions as well as political and historical experiences. This is especially good for children with LD, where hands-on experience as well as field trips are especially helpful. Additionally, if situations permit, city children can walk or take public transportation to and from school.

Country Schools

On the other hand, city schools do not have the vast openness of a country school, which usually has a park-like setting with miles of trails, athletic fields, and classroom and dorm buildings. Also, children at country schools are outdoors each day, and usually face fewer dangers to their personal safety than children on the streets of major American cities. On the other hand, field trips to historical, cultural and city activities may be fewer and farther apart.

Preprofessional Schools

One type of special-needs school is the preprofessional school for gifted youngsters with talents in the arts. These are similar to magnet schools which public schools may offer. Although your child has some form of LD, your child may also be gifted, requiring a school that specializes in the particular gifted arts program in which your child excels. These schools literally keep the child in a sociocultural vacuum, children spend the majority of their time practicing and learning their art rather than academics. Many times conventional education is received from a private tutor. Although many of the students who attend may develop into world-class artists, they often know little else but their art. Depending on the learning disability that your child has, this may suit your child very well. After all, the preprofessional school has focused its strengths on your child's strengths and, if successful, a meaningful career can develop. They will also have learned to deal with their disability. You cannot ask for much more than that. However, one problem still remains: the acceptance rate for these schools is usually low and competition is high.

If you want a more well-rounded student or if your child's disability is such that extra help or tutoring as well as therapy are needed, then you may want to consider a regular private school and devote your child's spare time to professional training.

It is important for you to investigate the claims any private school makes about its preprofessional training. Remember that most schools offer drama, art and music. That does not mean they are preprofessional caliber. If preprofessional training is important to you and your child, check with professionals in the world of drama, art and music to see if they can genuinely recommend the schools you are considering. If you do not know anyone in those fields, call the admissions department of some of the more famous schools such as Juilliard School of Music in New York City, the Ringling School of Art in Sarasota, Florida, the Rhode Island School of Design in Providence, Rhode Island, or the Yale Drama School in New Haven, Connecticut. Above all else, do not force or coerce your child into a preprofessional school, thinking that it will substitute for the LD that your child has. Remember, once LD, always LD; you and your child just need to learn how to handle it.

Postgraduate

Many private schools of all kinds – day, boarding, religious and military offer a 13th grade or postgraduate (PG) level. For the child with LD this is a godsend because it allows the student an additional year to achieve his or her academic potential before going off to college, vocational school, military training or entering the work force. It also allows an extra year for maturing. This extra year may be the difference between finishing the next level of schooling or not. Always ask private schools if they offer a postgraduate level. You may not need it, but at least it is there if you should.

Coed versus Single-sex Schools

Approximately, 78 percent of private schools are coed

where boys and girls share classes and all other educational opportunities. According to a recent study by the American Association of University Women Educational Foundation, schools remain "places of unequal opportunity," where girls face discrimination from teachers, textbooks, tests and male classmates. The study applied primarily to public schools. However, some gender bias creeps in the daily lives of even our finest coed private schools. And each time it usually benefits the boys. A solution to this dilemma is single-sex schools which free students of most sexual distractions and leave them far more able to concentrate on their schoolwork. Single-sex schools are especially helpful in allowing girls to excel in math, science and other predominantly male-oriented classes as well as leadership roles.

In addition to the other choices you will have to make about private schools, deciding the right environment for your child will depend largely on your child's own needs and how well you know those needs. But make certain your choice of school environment is based on your child's needs and not on your own.

Boarding Schools vs. Day Schools

The most obvious difference between a private day and boarding school is the number of hours spent in an educational environment. A private day school student has maybe seven or eight hours a day, five days a week in class, while in public school, class time is more like six hours a day, five days a week. Those short hours cannot be as effective in treating LD as a live-in faculty with a large corps of trained teachers who are in contact with the children throughout their waking hours, seven days a week. Boarding schools also teach and encourage independence, self-reliance, organizational skills and personal responsibility in ways which few parents can in a home setting, where a youngster can manipulate the environment more easily. For the child with LD, these are reasons enough to choose a boarding school.

You can easily compare a boarding school to a small town or village or walled community. You will usually find a church or chapel, if it has religious connections, a library, post office, barber shop, classrooms, a pool hall or recreation room, a staffed infirmary, a cemetery, a laundry, dry cleaners, cafeteria, snack bar, housing, auditorium, bus and van transportation, garage, music hall, little theater, community band, a jazz band, artist studio, miles of biking and walking paths, parks, lakes and streams, stables, firetruck(s), lots of recreational fields from football to baseball to lacrosse to soccer, a gymnasium, fitness center, pool and tennis courts. Some even have their own golf courses! As you can see, a boarding school does not lack for amenities. When it comes to academics, athletics and extracurricular activities, most boarding schools are better prepared than towns with populations of 25,000!

All schools, both public and private, have rules and regulations and boarding schools are no exception. Because boarding school students and faculty live in close quarters, students are forced to learn self-discipline and respect for the laws that govern their school. Boarding school students also learn that while living in small quarters 24 hours a day under the watchful eye of teachers, staff, counselors and administrators, nothing goes unnoticed. Conforming to rules and regulations is part of growing into adulthood. As a result, boarding school students emerge from their education far more confident and mature than the friends and other siblings that they left back home.

For all the blessings that boarding schools have, they also have negatives. For starters, just the cost of sending a child to boarding school is enormous! Boarding schools cost five times more than parochial schools and at least twice that of an expensive private day school. That just covers the tuition, room and board. Transportation costs are additional and many times your child will be traveling during peak travel times such as Thanksgiving, Christmas and Easter. Also, many boarding schools are situated in rural areas, away from metropolitan areas, so you will have additional costs in getting your child to a major transportation site. The boarding schools will take your child to the transportation site, but they may charge you a fee for doing so. In addition to transportation charges, most private schools have a dress code that will include expensive coats and ties for the boys and Sunday dress for the girls.

Spending money, though, will probably be less than when your child is living at home, since the child will not have as many temptations to buy. For the older child who has a driver's license, having a car is the ultimate dream. Boarding schools vary on the rules and regulations allowing students permission to have cars on campus, so that may be an additional break and less pressure for you. Also, if your child attends a boarding school without a car but has a driver's license, he or she may be classified as an occasional driver with your insurance company; therefore, you may not have excessively high insurance rates. Check with your insurance agent since many insurance companies offer lower rates to occasional drivers — especially boys.

If the boarding school you select accepts students who qualify as "handicapped" under PL 94-142, and the school accepts only learning disabled students, then you may qualify for tax savings because the tuition may be deductible. Medical care expenses are listed under Section 213 of the Internal Revenue Code. The regulation under Section 213 of the IRC provides that while ordinary education is not medical care, the cost of medical care includes the cost of attending a special school for a handicapped individual if his or her condition is such that the resources of the institution for alleviating such handicap are a principle reason for his or her presence there.

Whether tuition and other related expenses of the special school will be deductible in a particular case, however, will depend upon the facts and circumstances of each individual student's situation. There are also percentage limitations applicable to otherwise deductible medical expenses, depending on the parent's income. Therefore, before taking a tax deduction for expenses relating to the special education of your child, parents should consult the IRS, their CPA and/or tax attorney about the rulings and regulations under Section 213 of the Internal Revenue Code and other applicable law.

Although your child may qualify for tuition tax deductions and related expenses under the IRS ruling, this does not help the cash-flow problems that you may have as a result of sending your child to a boarding school. Tuition is steep, so be prepared. Many boarding schools are as sophisticated as colleges and universities in raising funds for their endowment, which is used to offer scholarships. Check with the schools you are considering for scholarship availability. Also, keep in mind that if you take the deductions, they must be for the calendar year, so, you will have to make full tuition payments by December 31, even though it may be more desirous to spread your tuition payments over the school year.

In addition to costs, the separation of the child and the parent, as well as the siblings who stay behind, can be painful. Not all children and families adapt to such separation, and some children have become so homesick that they become physically ill, and, many times, they cannot cope with the homesickness. This, unfortunately, does not just happen to the child. Parents, too, have become so homesick for the presence of their child that they have ended up in therapy. A solution to parental homesickness is to visit your child often and send lots of care packages. Even if they do not eat the "goodies" in the care packages, children learn at an early age to barter with their classmates, and food is the usual trade! The first time I sent my son, Dan, off to boarding school, I spent the next few months totally redecorating his room. I did all the painting and wallpaper myself, since this was *my* therapy. Of course, I had Dan approve of the colors and wallpaper and Dan, on vacation from school, was very happy to return home to a totally new room.

Most parents probably think that boarding schools are for high school students and not for young children. Wrong! There are boarding schools for children as young as eight and maybe even younger. You must wonder, why would a parent want to send his or her child off to boarding school so young? Well, if that were the best educational opportunity available, especially for the child with LD, why would you *not* think about sending your child? My son was sent off at the age of nine, and I cried for three weeks, but after I visited him and found him so happy and contented, I knew it was the right thing to do. For the first time, he was actually *learning*. The separation was extremely painful, but knowing that your child is learning, happy and his self-esteem is growing, what more can a mother ask?

There is one more drawback — not being able to share the joys, the tears and the laughter of guiding your adolescent through his or her teenage years. The sudden absence of a bubbling 14-year-old at home can be devastating. So, before settling on a boarding school, make sure both you and the child are ready for some separation.

Evaluating Private Schools

After comparing the various options which private day and boarding schools offer, the next question is where to begin finding schools both nearby and away from home. Finding a local private school is fairly easy – just look in the *Yellow Pages*. Further, ask other parents, teachers, guidance counselors and professionals who have tested your child for their recommendation. Check with clergy, friends and family members for references.

After getting a positive reaction to the local private school(s), make a quick telephone call to find out if LD classes are offered before setting up an appointment or investigating further. Many times schools will have students answer the telephone, so when calling, ask to speak with a guidance counselor, registrar or admissions counselor. As for boarding schools, several guides are available at your public library or you can order and purchase them at the local book store (see suggested readings, at the end of this chapter). Several of these guides also cover day schools.

Educational Consultants

Another more expensive route is hiring an educational consultant who can find and suggest both day and boarding schools. Look through the *Yellow Pages* under *Educational Consultants*, and you will find a list. Anyone can declare himself or herself an educational consultant since there is no college major or special schools to attend, neither are there any certifications or licensing professional qualifications. Unfortunately, as in other professions, there are people who are no more an educational consultant than Bart Simpson. However, there is one yardstick that you can use in finding a good educational consultant. Use a consultant who is a member of the Independent Educational Consultants Association (IECA). IECA membership is the only assurance you have of a consultant's professional qualifications. To get the names of consultants, contact IECA in Fairfax, Virginia, phone (703) 591-4850.

Educational consultants can charge more than $1,000 per client, which may or may not include testing. The fees are usually paid up front at the initial meeting. Most professional educational consultants have an intimate knowledge of a great percentage of private schools available, especially boarding schools. Even if they are not familiar with a particular school, they will do the research into that school as well as suggest possible other schools. During the first appointment, the consultant will be asking both you and your child many questions. Many of these questions I have already covered, such as coed versus single-sex schools, boarding versus day. In many cases, the consultant will have your child tested again, just to make sure he or she has full understanding of the disability. The whole idea behind using a consultant is to try to secure a good match between the child and the school, as well as the parents and the school.

A second appointment will be needed to explain the testing results and what type of schooling would be most appropriate for your child. The consultant will also have brochures from the recommended list of schools and maybe even some videos and tapes from the school. Once you agree on several schools to visit, the consultant will make the appropriate appointments.

The advantages of a good consultant are many. The time factor alone may be well worth the fee. The number of good boarding and day schools is astonishing. Finding the right match is no simple task. The consultant can help simplify the task and reduce the list from hundreds to just a few. If you do not like any of those choices, the consultant can come up with another list of possibilities. The consultant will also recommend schools where your child will have a chance at gaining admission. Admission is not guaranteed, but there is a very good chance that all the schools your consultant recommends will accept your child. However, whether you use a consultant or not, you will still need to visit the school and go through the interviewing process.

In the case of my son, I used an educational consultant and would recommend hiring one, especially if both parents are working and do not have the time to adequately concentrate in finding the right school for their child with LD.

At this point in the evaluation process, you should have narrowed the field down to schools according to single-sex versus coed, military, religious, country versus city, day versus boarding. Now the process is to narrow the choice even more without even setting foot on the campus. Begin by gathering all the brochures and other information packets you can from each of the schools you wish to investigate.

Accreditation and Certification

One of the first things to look for in the brochures is whether or not the schools in question are *accredited*. Accreditation is not the same as certification, and do not let anyone try to confuse you by using the term synonymously. Every state requires every school to be certified whether it is religious, private or public. Certification is nothing more than legal approval to operate. Depending on state laws, certification may only mean adherence to life safety laws.

On the other hand, accreditation is the result of complex examination conducted every one to ten years by the appropriate regional accreditation association (facing page). Each

Regional School Accreditation Commissions

Middle States Association of Colleges and Schools (MSACS)
(DE, DC, MD, NJ, NY, PA) Phone (215) 662-5600

New England Association of Schools and Colleges (NEASC)
(CT, ME, MA, NH, RI, VT) Phone (617) 271-0022

North Central Association of Colleges and Schools (NCACS)
(AZ, AK, CO, IL, IN, IA, KS, MI, MN, MO, NE, NM, ND, OH, OK, SD, WV, WI, WY)
Phone (800) 525-2517

Northwest Association of Schools and Colleges (NASC)
(AK, ID, MT, NV, OR, UT, WA) Phone (208) 334-3210

Southern Association of Colleges and Schools (SACS)
(AL, FL, GA, KY, LA, MS, NC, SC, TN, TX, VA) Phone (404) 679-4500

Western Association of Schools and Colleges (WASC)
(CA, HI, Guam and the Pacific Islands) Phone (415) 375-7711

Additional Accreditation Programs
Assn. of Independent Schools in New England, Phone (617) 849-3080
Assn. of Independent Colorado Schools, Phone (303) 442-5252
Assn. of Independent Maryland Schools, Phone (410) 987-7025
California Assn. of Independent Schools, Phone (310) 393-5161
Connecticut Assn. of Independent Schools, Phone (203) 572-2950
Florida Council of Independent Schools, Phone (813) 287-2820
Georgia Accrediting Commission, Phone (706) 542-3343
Independent Schools Assn. of Central States, Phone (708) 971-3581
Independent Schools Assn. of the Southwest, Phone (917) 921-7788
New York State Assn. of Independent Schools, Phone (518) 274-0184
North Carolina Office of Non-public Instruction, Phone (919) 733-4276
Pennsylvania Assn. of Private Academic Schools, Phone (215) 436-7429
Virginia Assn. of Independent Schools, Phone (804) 740-2643

association puts together teams of respected educators from other schools in the region to visit a particular school and examine its educational goals and standards. Accreditation is voluntary and granted only to schools meeting the minimum standards of each regional association.

In addition to meeting accreditation standards by one of the regional associations, any school you consider not supported by church or tax monies or any school that calls itself independent, should also belong to the National Association of Independent Schools (NAIS). They can be contacted at 1620 L Street, NW, Washington, D.C. 20036, phone (202) 973-9700. NAIS is a voluntary membership organization, and not all schools that apply qualify. The main point is that the schools you consider must be accredited, at the very least, by the regional accreditation, and if they are also accredited by another organization or two that is a plus for that school. Finding out if the school is accredited is simple – just ask. Accredited schools are proud of this and usually will have it printed on their brochures.

Academic Strengths

Other items to check into via brochures are the schools' academic strengths. Schools are always very proud of their academics and usually will brag about their students' academic rankings. However, you need to know how the schools' academic strengths relate to your child's ability.

Do not get caught in the trap of thinking that sending your child to an academically superior school, where he or she can mingle with academically gifted students will help his or her LD. Before deciding to send your child to an academically challenging school for intellectual stimulation, reread Chapter 2 on self-esteem! Chances of helping your child achieve academic success at such a school are slim at best. Remember, you are trying to find the best match and the best school for your child. You should be looking for a school where he or she can achieve. Being at the bottom of the class or bringing down the class average does nothing for self-esteem. In fact, if anything it leaves the child with a devastating feeling of being a failure. This is not what you want nor is it fair for your child to have to feel that way.

Extracurricular Activities

Beyond academics, private schools try to emphasize one or more areas of extracurricular activities and may have even built a reputation in one of those areas. One school may have a particularly good fine arts department. If your child is interested in any of these areas, further investigation may be warranted. Athletics is another area of specialization. There is one boarding school in Virginia that seven Heisman trophy winners have attended. That school definitely specializes in football. The point is to read the brochure carefully and check out the pictures. If the school specializes in an area that may be of valuable interest to your child, continue the investigation.

Student Profiles

The type of student admitted is also a consideration. Again, look at the profiles and pictures of the students in the brochure or catalog. If you think your child will do better in a school where there is not much diversity, then be certain that your child matches the description of the typical child in such a school.

On the other hand, if you prefer a more heterogeneous student body, try to find a school where your child will fit in academically, socially and emotionally. Pick a school where your child will have a comfortable peer group. When actually visiting the school, you can see first hand who the typical student is and be able to ask them questions.

Accreditation, extracurricular activities and student body make up are three areas you can determine from reading or looking at the brochure or catalogs. But do not be *too* impressed with the brochures. Remember, the schools are trying to sell their educational values to you, so do not be misled by all the slick pictures and videos. Schools are now sending prospective parents "Hollywood" type productions as a way to entice you to send your child to their school. Do not be bowled over by the video!

Visiting the Private School

The final step in the evaluation process is the actual visit to the school. If you are visiting pre-kindergarten through third grade, visit and interview the school by yourself. *Do not* take your child. The decision as to which school your child attends should be yours and not your child's. No matter how mature you think your preschooler is, do not take him or her to visit any school during your preliminary decision-making process. The selection of any school for this age group needs to be made by the parent. Only after you have made your decision should you show the new school to your child.

For late elementary levels, use your own judgment. If your child is extremely mature, then by all means have him/her accompany you to the school on your first visit. Middle schoolers and high schoolers should accompany you to the school on the first visit.

To set up your visit, just call or write to the school with

the dates on which you are available for appointments. Make sure at the time of the interview you will be able to tour the school as well as meet the headmaster and possibly sit in on one or two classes. If you are coming from a distance, let the school know that you are unable to come back for a second or third visit. Also, set up an appointment with the appropriate LD specialist(s) and/or therapist for an interview. If your child needs any therapy or excels in a specialized area such as music, art or sports, set up appointments with those teachers and coaches. When setting up the appointment, ask about how much time would be involved so that you can plan your day accordingly. A half day would probably be satisfactory, but in some cases you may want to stay for lunch, visit a sporting event or listen to a music class. Do not try to crowd too many schools into one visit. Visiting private schools is much different than interviewing the public schools. To really get a feel for a school you need to be on campus for several hours, not just asking questions but also touring the campus and seeing the students in action.

The Interview Process

The interview process can be divided into five parts: the interview as a family, with parents only, with just the prospective student, a campus tour and possibly some student testing. Not all schools will test; some may accept previous school records and tests, especially if the scores are recent. Rarely do all five steps take place, but usually at least three of them will, so be prepared. You may want to wait until you have definitely decided on a school or two before requesting that the previous school records be sent. What you may want to do is take a recent report card or test scores to the interview with you. At the appropriate time, you may want to share them with the admissions counselor. If you have used an educational consultant, the consultant can send the necessary test results in advance to the admissions counselor.

Also, no matter what the age, prepare your child for the visit. The admissions representative will probably want to talk to the child without the parents present, so prepare the child for that. The admission counselor just wants to hear the student's opinion of the school, nothing formal, just plain and simple. Does the student want to attend this school? Does the student want to go away from home? What is the bonding between parent and child? That is what the counselor is looking for.

When we went for an interview for the first time, we were taken to a comfortable sitting room. It had a long couch and several overstuffed chairs. I immediately went for the couch, followed by our son and my husband. At first, I thought we probably looked a little odd as all three of us were sitting on the couch together rather than spread out, but, on the contrary, that was exactly what the admissions counselor wanted to see: a family together and not divided with the parents on one side of the room and the child on the other. We passed the interview just from that sitting arrangement!

When you visit the school, keep an open mind. Do not be overly impressed with shining new buildings, great dorms and lots of playing fields. Those things will help sell the school but should not influence your decision from the beginning. Your goal of every visit should be to find the right match for your child. Admissions counselors are professional and are eager to admit students who will succeed and be happy, productive members of their student body. They are not trying to keep students out but trying to find students who fit their mold.

If they tell you they feel their school would not be a good

match, do not take it personally. Admissions counselors are well-trained educators, and they want students who will succeed and leave their school with their self-esteem intact. If they feel your child would not do well, they probably will suggest other schools, and if they do not suggest other schools, ask which schools they feel would fit your child's learning style. Most admissions counselors cannot afford bad advice since their school and their own professional reputation are on the line. So take their advice and pursue their recommendations.

Your Questions for the Initial Interview

The following are questions that you need to ask each school. As you read over each question, picture how it relates to your child's LD problem(s) and why it is important. You need only to ask the pertinent questions that relate to your child, and I recommend writing them down on index cards so you can note your opinions on the card after each question.

What is the educational philosophy of the school?

Clearly stated goals are important for faculty, staff, students and parents. First of all, they give the faculty and staff a clear policy for working with students. Second, they tell students what is expected of them, and third, they give you and other parents a chance to compare the school's goals with your own. If the differences are too great, take your child elsewhere. If the school is serious about LD support, it will be stated in the school philosophy. If it is missing from the educational philosophy, then I would seriously question just how important a role LD plays with the school in question!

What are the rules and regulations to which each child is expected to adhere ?

If structure is important to you, then here is where to find out just how structured and disciplined the school is. You need to know what type of punishments are used and who enforces the rules. Is it peers, administrators, teachers, counselors or faculty advisors? In today's society, where sex, drugs and alcohol are easily accessible, how does the school combat these social ills and does the school have a program of education on chemical and drug dependency? Also, if the student is caught with drugs or alcohol, what is the consequence? Many schools will say automatic expulsion while others will give a second chance. How do you as parents want it to be handled? Another question is the smoking policy for both students and faculty. Again, decide if the way rules are applied by the school is the way you want your child treated. The decision is up to you.

Communications — How much and what kind of communications are there between parents, teachers and school?

How does the school keep parents informed about their child's academic and social development? What is the frequency, and is it done informally, in person, via phone or weekly reports? Is there a calendar of events for the full year or do they make it out month to month? How much access do you as parents have to your child's teachers? Are parents welcome on campus at any time?

What are the teaching requirements needed to teach at this school?

Most schools have a published list of their faculty along with their educational credentials. What percentage of teachers are tenured or retained each year? If there is a high turnover, you may want to "red flag" that area. Ask the number that have masters or higher degrees, and check out the colleges they attended. Did they come from one college or university in particular? Some religious schools will hire only teachers from a college or university of the same faith. Is that important to you, or do you want a school that has a more diversified faculty? If it is a boarding school, do faculty live on campus or in the dorms? What percentage live on or near the campus? Do the faculty who live on campus have campus duties in addition to teaching? If so, what are they? If they have too many additional responsibilities, they may not have enough time for teaching.

What is the financial position of the school?

Now this is a "tricky" but most important question to ask. There are several reasons why you should ask this question and the most important is that, next to the family, the school plays a very important role in children's lives. To children, school signifies a stabilizing force. If the school collapses, then children are forced to attend a new school, possibly without their friends. For some children, this can be a devastating event. But there are ways to ask this question without prying into private financial matters of the school.

First, ask if there is an endowment, and if so, find out its size and how long it has been in existence. Other subjects about which you should ask include the long-term and short-term building goals – when was the last capital campaign and what was it for? When is the next capital campaign scheduled and for what purpose? Also check out what the enrollment projections are for the next three to four years as well as what the previous years' enrollment figures were. Finally, check out the teacher/student ratios for previous years as well as what is forecast. All of these things can tell you if the school is working within a well-maintained budget or are they just scrimping to get by. You are looking for growth and stability at the school.

How safe is the school socially as well as physically?

Today our streets, homes, businesses, churches, and schools are not safe from local petty crime as well as more serious crime, and the 1997-1998 school year saw more guns and violence in schools across the nation than ever before. Asking about the safety of the school is certainly not out of the question. Again, check out the neighborhood. If the surrounding neighborhood is slum-filled, will that spill over to the campus? If it is a city school, is the school "walled in" to protect from outside trespassers? Who greets the children each morning as they arrive, and who supervises the departing students? If the school is a boarding school, how safe are the dormitories from outside trespassers? Do students have keys to lock their rooms? Are the dorms locked at night and if so, at what time and who keeps the keys?

Fire and environmental safety is also important to touch on. If the buildings are old, ask about asbestos and lead poisoning. Are fire drills practiced routinely and documented? If a boarding school, ask if fire drills are held at night. Ask these questions before enrolling, and if the school cannot answer your questions satisfactorily, find a school that can.

If the school is both day and boarding ask what the percentage is of each. If it is a boarding school, is it five or seven day boarding?

If your child will be a boarder, and more than 50 percent are day students, find a school that has a much higher percentage of boarders. The reverse is also true. If your child will be a day student at a boarding school, you should look for a school that has mostly day students. Boarding schools offer either a seven-day boarding program or a five-day boarding program, and there are some that have both. If the boarding school is both, ask what the percentage breakdown is. If your child will be there seven days, you want the greater percentage of students attending seven days. And the reverse holds true. Many five-day boarding schools are located near large metropolitan areas, where students board for five days even though they may live within a 50-mile radius from school. They usually spend the weekends at home. Check out the rules that permit five-day boarding. Do students have to earn merits in order to go home for weekends or do anything special to get weekend passes? Can seven-day boarders visit five-day boarders on weekends at their homes?

If a boarding school, ask:
What weekend activities are scheduled
and available for students?
Are there additional fees associated with the activities?

Ask to see the published list of activities for a particular month. Make sure there are enough activities so each child can choose among several weekend events. Ask how the residential staff is selected and ask if there is a separate activities staff for anything which falls in the category of extracurricular. Most importantly, how often do students go home for the weekend? If it is a great percentage and you live hundreds of miles away, this may not be a good situation for your child. Also, what extra fees are required for these extracurricular activities?

The whole interview should not last over 30 to 40 minutes, since all of these questions should be answered fairly easily without the counselor having to look up any answers. While asking the questions, you should feel fairly confident and at ease, because you are controlling the discussion. However, the counselor will be interviewing *you*, as well.

The School's Staff, Observing Classes
and the Campus Tour

After the initial interview is over, ask to meet with any LD staff, especially the director of the LD program. I would also insist on observing or sitting in on one or two of the classes. This should have been arranged at the time of the interview but if not, ask now. Any good LD program director will want to meet you and the potential student. If he or she does not have the time or interest in meeting you, I would question whether or not there is actually an LD director. Do not let the director use only test scores to determine if your child is eligible for LD classes. If the director does not have the time to meet you and your child, look elsewhere! If the director of the LD program is serious about the program, he or she will make time to visit with you, if only for a few minutes.

If your child has any special talents or special interests such as sports, music, art or photography, be sure to tell the admissions counselor that you would like to meet with the director in the area of interest. If the school boasts that it rates superior in a certain area and that is an area of interest to your child, then you should be able to meet with the director. If there is no one person in charge of that program, then I would suggest you find another school with that specialty. Obviously, the school you are interviewing is not serious or does not have the resources if there is no one person responsible for that area.

After all these interviews, a campus tour would be in order. Usually, in middle and upper schools, tours will be conducted by students from the grade that your child would be in. At the lower level, usually the director or another faculty member gives the tour. This is a win-win situation for you and your child. You can actually speak to someone who will probably give you the very frank answers and not just a "canned" sales pitch. If a student is giving the tour, you can ask all sorts of questions on subjects ranging from dorm life to social development to their personal opinion of the school. If it is a faculty member, ask what it is really like to teach on campus or what makes this school shine over another school? The questions can be endless, and you will probably get more honest answers from the student or teacher than the ones from the admission counselors.

While on tour, remember to ask many questions and peek in as many nooks and crannies as possible. Observe the cleanliness of the overall campus. While walking halls and classrooms, pay attention to the lighting and if student work is displayed. Are the classes structured with every desk and chair in a perfect row, or are there group dynamics going on with students? How big are the classes? Is there some order or is there chaos? Finally, as you pass students, staff and faculty on the campus, do they seem friendly, stopping to say hello or to introduce themselves? This can really reveal the personality of the school.

In what shape are the structures?

Obviously, this can be seen on the tour, but look over buildings for maintenance and cleanliness. Also observe the grounds and building exteriors. Is the schoolyard safe, attractive and well maintained? Is the fencing in good shape? Maintenance can tell the whole story. If there is a maintenance department, talk to an employee in that area. If it is a large school, how many maintenance people are there? Is the paint chipping? Are there leaky roofs? Are the restrooms clean? Just look it all over — like buying a house — peek wherever you can.

What type sports are offered during the year?

Determine not only what sports are offered but also the condition of the gym, playing fields and equipment. At middle and upper schools there should be adequate facilities for intramural as well as varsity and junior varsity programs for interscholastic competition. Also, if sports are important to you, talk with the athletic director (AD). Ask how many students participate and if everyone gets a chance to play a sport. In other words, are they "bench warmers." Ask how often games are scheduled, and are they on weekends or weekdays? You might as well address the bus issue. How are the buses maintained and/or do they bring in rentals for away games or do they transport in vans or school buses?

What type of extracurricular activities are offered?

Depending on your child's interest, ask to see other areas such as the music room, band, newspaper, yearbook or darkroom. If your child is not into music, then do not make a production out of seeing the music room. Throughout the interview keep your questions focused on your child and your child's interests.

Be sure to check the cafeteria, infirmary, lockers and any other facilities that may affect your child's life.

There are all sorts of questions associated with the cafeteria. You should ask about the menus – quality as well as quantity. How it is served: cafeteria, sit down or family style? Can the students sit anywhere? Is milk offered? May students go back for seconds? Your child may be just as anxious to hear the answer to these questions as you are. I am sure they will have even better questions. For boarding students, ask if they have three full meals on weekends as well as during the week. Also, do students have to dress a particular way for meals? Is there an entrée selection? What about special diets – vegetarian, low fat, salad bars, dessert bars?

If it is a boarding school, is there a nurse available 24 hours a day, just in case your child may need medical attention. As a parent, you know that most children do not tell you they are sick, coming down with a cold or injured themselves, until late at night when everything is closed. It would be nice to know that someone would be available to help your child if the need arose.

For a boarding school, visit the dorm area, especially the dorm where your child may be placed. Ask about roommates.

Dorms come in all sizes, shapes and conditions. Pay close attention to the lifestyle in the dorms. Are there locks on the doors? Where are the showers and bathrooms? Hot water? Who cleans the rooms and washrooms? What about laundry and

Tips for Parents of Boarding Students

When you send your child off for the first time to a boarding school, the school will send a list of items you should bring. My experience with boarding schools has found that the school's list is incomplete, so I am offering a baker's dozen of specific suggestions:

Clothes – Buy as much as you can of cotton and/or acrylic clothes, linens and blankets. Otherwise, you may end up with a huge dry cleaning bill.

Cords – Space is limited and there are few electrical outlets. Bring extension cords, better yet a 6-plug outlet;

First-aid kit – Should contain nonperishable and nonprescription items only, such as adhesive bandages, cotton balls, cough drops, whatever your child uses at home.

Disposables – Include trash bags, light bulbs, tissues and several paper towel rolls.

Cleaners – Choose a bottle of glass cleaner and/or a general cleanser and, most importantly, a large container of disinfectant – this may help to keep the germs to a minimum.

Fasteners – Plastic-tac or Funtac for fastening items to the walls.

Laundry bag – or hamper.

Pack seasonal – Closet space is limited and clothes can be changed during break periods.

For the high school student who needs to wear dress pants and sport coats or the young lady who must wear dresses – there are two items on the market today which are costly but can save in dry cleaning bills as well as the wear and tear on clothes. One is a pants presser and the other is a streamer. Both cost around $150 but can last a lifetime. Using such items also teaches children to take care of their clothes and gets them in the habit of looking neat and clean.

Most importantly: DON'T BRING A TRAILER FULL OF THINGS THEY CAN'T LIVE WITHOUT BECAUSE THEY CAN – SPACE IS AT A PREMIUM!

dry cleaning? As you visit the room, check to see how it is furnished. Can you bring furniture to school? What about stereos, mini refrigerators, fans, microwaves? Is there a central kitchen so that food can be stored? What are the rules attached to dorm life? Can you put pictures on the wall? Bedspreads and linens? And an important issue for your child is the phone — how many, how long, how often! These questions just cut the surface. Once a decision is made to attend a boarding school, check your local library for books on the subject. I have included at the end of this chapter some ideas on what to bring and not to bring to boarding schools.

Go With Your Feelings

After all the interviews, the testing and the campus tour, the real decision to attend or not can be made from your own feelings. You have asked all the correct questions. The school has accepted you, but you still have an uneasy feeling. You do not need a reason to like or dislike a school, but you need a feeling that you have found the best school for your child at this time. You may find that after a year at one particular school you will need to look for another school. Children outgrow schools as they outgrow shoes, so do not think that once you find that perfect fit you can relax because no sooner than you do that, you will find your child has outgrown that perfect little school, also. Good luck!

In a Nutshell . . .

—   Before beginning to search for the private school, have an idea of which of the following types of schools you might be interested in: the basic day private, military, religious, and/or boarding school.

—   Also figure out if you are interested in a coed school.

—   For possible tax savings, check with the school that you are considering and also check with your CPA/tax attorney to see if you qualify under the Internal Revenue Code under Section 213.

—   Before starting to narrow the list of schools to consider for your child with LD, keep in mind that a school that is "perfect" for one child may not be so for another child, even in the same family. There are no perfect schools — only schools that may be best for your child, and only you and your child can determine that.

—   When it comes to finding the perfect private day school for your child with LD, you may find that choices may be overwhelming. But again, ask questions, visit the school and interview the headmaster. Notice the name change — headmaster. In boarding schools as well as day schools, the principal is now the headmaster.

—   Ultimately, go with your "gut" feeling. You do not need a reason to dislike a school. If your intuitive feeling says this is not the school, look elsewhere.

Frequently Asked Questions
Concerning Private Day and Boarding Schools

Why should I pay for a private school education for my child with LD when there are good public schools available?

You shouldn't. If your school district has a good public school that your child can attend, and that same school offers the appropriate LD support that will help your child, then I would not even bother looking into private education, if I were you. The point of this book is to give parents options in the education of their child. Private day and boarding schools and home schooling are available options when public schools cannot offer the help that your child may require.

How do you know if your child will benefit from a post-graduate year?

You never know for sure if the entire year will be wasted or if it will be beneficial. An added year would definitely help mature the child before entering vocational school, community college, college, the armed services or the workplace. But don't think that the additional year will help your child get over LD; once LD always LD.

Will using tax incentive Section 213 of the IRS Code cause our taxes to be automatically audited?

Who knows for sure? According to one accountant, it would probably flag your return but would not automatically cause an audit of your return unless there were other considerations that were also flagged. In my case, I was audited not because of a Section 213 deduction, but due to other circumstances. Of course, when they saw that I had also used Section 213, I was questioned. I delivered, in a sealed envelope, the psychologist's report and asked that it be kept confidential. It was, and it was returned to me within 24 hours with no further questions asked. That was five years ago, and I have not been audited since.

My child is LD and now becoming a discipline problem. Will boarding school help?

Do not think for one moment that a boarding school is there to handle only discipline problems. They will work with you, but my experience with boarding schools is that they are there to help you, and together they will help your child. But your child must be willing to work with the school in solving any discipline problems, otherwise, you are throwing away your money. It is true that in years past, military schools and Catholic schools would use strict discipline to control and/or make children act accordingly. However, today schools are faced with many more problems than discipline, and, as a result, problem delinquents are not always welcomed at boarding or private day schools. Be up front with the school.

Is it really worth using an Educational Consultant?

It is my experience that it is worth it if you find one who understands your needs. I have to admit, the first time I used one, I was very skeptical, but after one visit I knew that it was worth every penny. I have continued to use the same consultant since then. But, again, you must find the right match for you an your child. The best place to start is to contact the Independent Educational Consultants Association (IECA) at

(703) 591-4850 for a list of consultants near your home. The IECA membership is the only assurance you have of a consultant's professional qualifications.

I just visited one of the most prestigious boarding schools in the Northeast, but for some reason I did not like it. However, since my child was accepted, I feel I should send her. What do you think?

Parents know their children better than any school board, administration, admission's counselor or teacher. If your "gut" feeling is that the school in question is not suitable for your child, go with your instinct. Don't feel you need a solid reason not to send your child to a particular school; rather, you want to find a school that will give your child the best education and support you can find. If you find yourself second-guessing a school, then that is not the one for your child. But be sure that the reason you did not like a particular school was not due to the thought of sending your child away to school. The decision to send the child is a weighty one, but you must analyze that decision separately from the decision to send the child to a particular school.

See also "Suggested Reading" for Chapter 8, p. 277.

Chapter 9

School Option #3: Homeschooling

Understanding Homeschooling

Although statistics are not readily available, most authorities believe that the number of children taught in homeschools across the nation is growing each year. In June, 1996, *Education Week* reported that homeschooling is becoming more "mainstream" – increasing, "not just in their numbers, but in the diversity of philosophies, politics and approaches represented in their burgeoning ranks." Homeschooling is beginning to be viewed as a "viable educational option." In Florida, for example, the homeschooled population has grown so fast over the years that the Department of Education (DOE) for the State of Florida has set up separate office just to handle inquiries, answer questions and assist families who homeschool.

A 1991 national survey by The National Home Education Research Institute, under the direction of Dr. Brian Ray, surveyed over 1,500 homeschooled families. The following are some of the findings from Dr. Ray's study.

—   The average age of the children in the families studied was just over eight years, and it appeared that the majority of the children had never been in public or private schools. There were an equal number of male and female children.

—   On standardized achievement tests, homeschooled students performed at or above the 80th percentile on national norms in terms of their reading, listening, language, math, science, social studies, basic battery and complete battery scores. The national average in conventional schools was the 50th percentile.

—   As for attending college, 33% homeschooled students went on to four-year colleges, 17% went to two-year colleges, and 17% went to college after waiting a year.

—   The average cost to homeschool was $488 per student per year.

As more and more parents become disillusioned with the traditional public school, they are turning to homeschooling. Historically, families who homeschooled did so more out of a religious conviction than any other reason. But in the 1994-95 school year, the Florida Department of Education surveyed homeschooled families and found that the reason most families homeschooled was not for religion, but dissatisfaction with the public school environment (safety, drugs and adverse peer pressure). The second reason given was dissatisfaction with public school instruction, and religious reasons placed third (Statistical Brief, Page 3). These are valid reasons for opting out of the traditional public school, but why are parents hopping into homeschooling?

Homeschooling Advantages

One of the main attractions to homeschooling, especially for the child with LD, is the ability to individualize your child's particular needs and to avoid the frustrations of trying to find the best school situation in the public school system or private sector. Through homeschooling, parents realize right away whether or not their child is learning, understanding and grasping what is being taught. No more worry or wondering if your child is "falling through the cracks." Instead, if one method of teaching does not work, then the parent/teacher has the option of trying another teaching style. Through hands-on teaching and self-adjusted teaching style, the parent/teacher can change to fit the learning style of the child. Homeschooling can be a great tutorial program with one-on-one learning that is tailored to meet your child's specific needs, pace and learning styles.

Another attraction to homeschooling is the opportunity for children to observe, first hand, their parents interacting in real-life situations. This helps to develop the social cues that children with LD often have a difficulty learning (see Chapter 2, "Self-Esteem and Social Development"). As a child watches his or her parent in everyday situations, from grocery shopping to mailing a package to answering the door bell, he/she observes the parent interacting with various people from all walks of life in various occupations. This gives your child a positive role model as well as the opportunity to build social skills. It teaches the child how to handle people, how to handle problems and helps the child mature naturally.

Another side effect of homeschooling is integrating theory with practical, everyday skills, such as cooking. What better way to teach basic math than to use a measuring cup and end up baking a cake? Or if fractions are being taught, order a hot pizza and divide it in eighths, fourths and so on. This certainly is an oversimplification of math, but you get the point. One homeschooled family built their dream house themselves and involved their three homeschooled children in the building process. This is a great way to learn about electricity, plumbing, geometry and life skills to last a lifetime! As a parent/ teacher, you have the flexibility to teach life skills from cooking to budgeting, from sewing to home maintenance, without leaving your home. Few would argue that there is a better role model than the parent to teach these life skills.

Parents also find homeschooling, especially for the child with LD, allows more hands-on experience than any public or private schooling could offer, and children are not restricted to what is available in their geographic area. An example of such an opportunity is: an Audubon Society chapter visiting homeschoolers across the state using examples from nature to teach academic skills (Grau). Another option is using on-line curriculum, which includes online assistance and communicating directly with astronauts on the space shuttle or scientists wintering in Antarctica (info-lfa@quest.arc.nasa.gov or Margaret Riel at InterLearnmriel@weber.ucsd.edu). And just recently, NBC's *The Today Show* featured a young family who sold their possessions, bought a motor home and are now visiting each state in the Union. The children, of course, are being homeschooled while traveling, but what better way to learn history, geography, geology, math and all other related subjects.

Also, as was mentioned in the chapter on public schools (see Chapter 7, "School Options #1: Public Schools"), not all schools are equal in regards to equipment. You may find that your household has a more sophisticated, as well as faster and more up-to-date computer system and software than the best school in your district. For the child with LD, computers are a wonderful teaching and learning instrument. For these children, becoming computer literate is not a choice or a luxury but an absolute necessity.

There are hundreds of places to visit when you are on the Internet that would be of particular interest to homeschooling families. There are sites with lesson plans, educational shareware, research libraries, support and discussion groups along with myriad projects in which your children can participate or contribute. Some of these programs may not be suitable for your child with LD, but as you surf the Internet you will find other families and other programs geared specifically to the homeschooler and child with LD. See the facing page for a basic listing of Internet resources for homeschoolers.

Researching Homeschooling

Parents who are not familiar with homeschooling often wonder how they can be a role model for their child 24 hours a day without losing their minds. The answer is simple: schedule socialization opportunities with your child's peers after school, on weekends, at church, at Little League or dance classes – the list never ends. There are plenty of social opportunities for your child to develop good socialization skills with his/her peers. Furthermore, as parent/teacher, you can be selective about the peer group in which your child interacts.

Internet Resources for Homeschoolers

Education Resources
http://paul.spu.edu/library/second/lc.html#Home*
Home and Alternative Schooling, Special Education, Talented and Gifted, Urban Education, Adult and Distance Education

Jon's Homeschool Page
http://www.midnightbeach.com/hs
News Groups, Mailing Lists, Generic Parenting Resources, Home Education Resources, Jewish Homeschooling Resources, Islamic Educational and Muslim Home School Resources

Home Schooling on Yahoo
http://www.yahoo.com/Business/Corporations/Education/Home_Schooling/
Searchable Database, Home Education Publishers of books and magazines, Educational placement testing and evaluation, Home Based Education Programs & Curriculum, Homeschool Guides, Organizations

The CEARCH Virtual Schoolhouse
http://sunsite.unc.edu/cisco/schoolhouse.html
A Meta-Library of K-12 Internet Links, Virtual Classrooms, Links to libraries and book-related sites, Virtual Art Room, Virtual Playground, Teaching resources on the Internet

Steve Mikulski's Technology Education Page
http://www.dsport.com/sjm/
Technology Education Resources, Journal of Technology Education, Education Mail Lists, K-12 Help/Resources

Jerome Graham's page
http://www.halcyon.com/jerome/home.html
Homeschooling Mailing Lists

home-ed@world.std.com
Subscribe: home-ed-request@world.std.com
Very active listserv

continued on the next page

Internet Reources for Homeschoolers continued from the previous page

home-ed-politics@mainstream.com
Subscribe: home-ed-politics-request@mainstream.com.
strong anti-government sentiments primarily from the Christian conservative/ libertarian/anarchist end of the spectrum.

homeschool_train_up_a_child@mainstream.com
Subscribe: hstuac@vms1.cc.uop.edu
forum for discussing the practical aspects of Christian homeschooling. No theological debates or political debates, digest availabl

TRAIN-UP-A-CHILD
Hub@XC.Org
with the message: subscribe TRAIN-UP-A-CHILD your@address.here
List to promote and encourage Christian Homeschoolers, also a list to help encourage in Christian parenting

Taking Children Seriously
listserv@netcom.com
Subscribe: TCS-list [your e-mail address]
This list, sponsored by Sarah Lawrence of the British homeschooling magazine is for discussion of what it means to raise children as human beings in their own right

The Unschooling Mailing List
majordomo@nilenet.com with
Subscribe: unschooling-list
Trusting a child's ability to learn and providing a stimulating and diverse environment define the essence of unschooling

Homeschooling News Groups

misc.education.homeschool.misc
A forum for the discussion of any and all aspects of homeschooling

misc.education.homeschool.christian
A forum specifically for Christian homeschooling families

Many more sources can be found by searching your internet service provider site (such as AOL) or using your web browser or one of the major search engines, with search strings such as "homeschooling AND learning AND disabilities".

Hopefully, should your child return to the public/private school setting, the values which your child has learned from the parent/teacher, as well as peers, are strong enough to endure any outside influences.

A frequent question that parents often ask is, "What are the qualifications to become a teacher to my child?" You may not have thought of this, but since the first time you held your child in your arms you have been a teacher to your child. Your child has been observing, watching, mimicking you since birth, it should not surprise you that parents are, in fact, teachers! Do you need a Ph.D. to homeschool? Hardly, nor do you need a master's degree – but what you do need is a lot of love for your child, flexibility, patience, sensitivity, organizational ability, a definite sense of humor, a desire to grow and learn, tenacity, determination, a desire to spend extended time with children, good family communications, a discipline plan that works, financial resources and space. If you possess these qualities, then you definitely have the ability to teach your child at home.

Most of those qualities are self-evident. But I would like to comment on the last two qualities – financial resources and space. First of all, homeschooling will be vastly less expensive than a private day and definitely not as much as boarding school. The cost can be up to you. New, grade-specific curriculum materials can range in price from under $100 to over $500 for all subjects. The most expensive will be prepackaged programs which provide extensive curriculum guides. If you decide to use a consultant to make up the curriculum, the average cost, say, for a fourth-grade curriculum would be $250, including the consultant's fee. A rule of thumb: the higher the grade level, the higher the price tag. Listed on the next page are several correspondence schools, which the State of Florida recognizes and which offer curriculum sup-

Curriculum Resources for Homeschoolers

American School
(high school)
Chicago, Il.
1-800-228-5600

Calvert School
Baltimore, Md.
K-8 Correspondence
301-243-6030

Extension School
University of Nebraska
(Independent Study)
Lincoln, Nebraska
402-472-1926

University of Florida
Correspondence Study
2209 NW 13th St.
Gainesville, Fl. 32609
904-392-1711 Ext. 200

port, guidance and prepackaged plans. Before signing with any of the correspondence schools (prepackaged plans), be sure you understand what you are paying for, that the curriculum will match your child's level, that it is recognized by your state and that it will work with your child's disability. When speaking with the educational consultants from each of these correspondence schools, make sure they fully understand the extent of your child's disability.

Do not feel that you *must* use the prepackaged curriculum. Check with your local school board for an outline of the curriculum in the grade that you will be teaching. Also, arrange to talk to an LD teacher from the school district who has experience for your child's grade level. Between the curriculum outline and the interview with the LD teacher, you should be able to mold the curriculum to fit your child's learning style and ability. Also check with your local school board and county library for dates when they give away used textbooks and outdated library books. You may also be able to borrow or exchange with other homeschools not only in your area but on the Internet, too. As you meet other homeschooling parents, you will learn of other unique and different plans for building curricula and your own library at home.

Your child with LD may also need additional tutoring as well as therapies. Tutoring varies in locales but will probably range from $20 and up per half hour, depending on the curriculum area. If you have a local community college or university, check with the education department office to see they have students who are interested in teaching children with LD. You may luck out and find a special college student who is anxious to tutor students with LD. This is a win-win situation for you. First, you are getting someone who could be a role model for your child as well as getting a good tutor fairly cheaply.

Understanding the Homeschooling Controversy

A recent controversy about homeschooled children concerns whether homeschooled children have the right to use or join public school facilities and/or activities. Public schools often allow students who are homeschooled to participate in band and drama clubs, but allowing them to participate in sports has caused some problems.

Public school parents object to homeschoolers competing with enrolled students for popular activities with limited enrollment, such as sporting events or band — especially when this privilege is not available to students in vocational and parochial schools. Homeschool parents, on the other hand, argue they are in the public school system because they follow the rules and regulations set up in the school district covering homeschooling, and they also pay their taxes.

Presently, eight states have passed legislation allowing homeschoolers to participate in sports, band and similar activities. Check with your local school board to see where they stand on this issue.

If your school system is receptive to after-school sports, they will probably allow you to use publicly funded therapy for your homeschooler, such as speech therapy, occupational therapy and/or physical therapy, since all three of these therapies are offered free of charge through the public school system. Even though you do not send your child to the local school system, you still pay property taxes, therefore, you should be eligible for therapy services. You will need to be flexible in working out a time slot with the school district. Remember, patience and flexibility are both attributes necessary to be a homeschool parent.

Another item that is needed is space. This does not mean you need to hire an architect to add rooms to your home. If you take some time to think about it, get a little creative and move a few items around, you probably will have space available. I know of one family who used office space at the father's veterinary office for homeschooling. The children went to school at their father's office with their mother as their teacher. Other families have converted their garage or used their dining room table for a desk and crates to store school supplies and books. So be a little creative.

As for other resources and items needed to set up a classroom in your home, I have included a beginner's checklist on the facing page. This may be a good way for you to determine how much the homeschool education option will cost. Remember, too, homeschooling your children may mean that you may be reduced to one pay check, which may be a problem if you are accustomed to the extra income of both parents working.

Researching the Laws and Getting Help

At this point, if you feel homeschooling is for you, check with the Department of Education (DOE) of your state regarding laws governing homeschooling. Laws vary from state to state and in some states from district to district. Some states will be more homeschool friendly than others, so be prepared. After contacting your state DOE for requirements and information, ask friends, neighbors and relatives for names of families which might be homeschooled. You may be surprised at how many parents in your city educate their children at home. They would be your best source for information in your search

Homeschool Materials List

Basic Supplies/Organization Helps
Desk with appropriate lighting
Bookshelves or storage crates
Filing cabinet or cardboard boxes
Answering machine and cordless phone or phone with a long cord
Blackboard and/or white wipe-off board or individual boards.
Two large, 3-ring binders (1 to keep records and 1 to keep each child's work)
Appointment book
Large calendar
Lesson plan book
Attendance calendar

Classroom Resources
World map, United States map, State map and a globe
Pencils, pens, erasers, chalk
Paper – lined and unlined
Science equipment

Books and References
Grade level curriculum & resources
Student dictionary and thesaurus (grade 3 and up)
Student atlas
English usage handbook (gr. 3 and up)
Encyclopedia set (or use the set at the library)

Technology
Computer (can use local library)
User-friendly word-processing software
Developmentally appropriate computer games / curriculum support software

Art Supplies
Plastic bins or shoe boxes to store art supplies
Construction paper
Scissors
Crayons
Felt-tipped pens
Watercolors/brushes
Glue stick
Liquid glue
Tempera paints
*You need to have on hand only the age-appropriate items for your child

to discover the pros and cons of homeschooling as well as the local laws and requirements. Finally, check with your own local school board. For the most part, the board will be helpful, but if they are not, do not get discouraged. There are groups out there which will help you, so you must keep looking, probing and asking lots of questions.

Support groups will also help you get started in homeschooling. They are a big benefit to homeschool families and they are a great way to make friends for your kids and you. Support groups can provide encouragement and information for new homeschoolers, revitalize seasoned homeschoolers and provide a set of people who share similar interests. They also provide a place for homeschooled children to meet other children and this is particularly important for teenagers. Support groups can also keep members informed on local, state and national political issues concerning homeschooling, as well as providing a network for field trips or even for team teaching. If there are two children studying the same concept, and one parent is more knowledgeable than another, then maybe that parent will volunteer to teach that subject while the other parent teaches something else. Support groups are nothing more than a source for the parent/teacher to gain support and encouragement from other parent/teachers, and they allow a sharing of ideas, materials, teaching strategies and concerns.

Usually several support groups exist in an area, so if the first one does not fit your lifestyle, look for others or form one of your own. Also, perhaps instead of an organized support group, three or four parents can get together on an informal basis or chat over the phone to discuss various items or concerns. The support group is for your benefit, so find one or start one that will agree with your likes. Remember, always keep asking questions and probing. Only then will you find your answers.

The information that I have presented on homeschooling for your child is just basic information and not nearly complete enough to even make a final decision as to whether you can or should homeschool your child. This information gives you an additional option, but you, the parent/teacher, must continue to look for additional information on this topic before making the final decision on whether to homeschool or not.

Homeschooling is an option, but it is not for everyone. You may possess all the qualifications, but there is one more qualification that is dearly needed if you are to homeschool your child, that is — *dedication.* If you decide to homeschool, it will be your career. It is a career in which you will be definitely underpaid and overworked, but the end result will be well worth it.

But being the parent/teacher is not that simple. The dedication that you will need to give to this career may be more than you can give, not because of a lack of knowledge or dedication, but because the frustrations and problems which you will face as a parent/teacher of your child with LD are not the same frustrations and problems which other parent/teachers experience.

Before you make your final decision, keep in mind that your child is LD and that you fully understand the disability and are on top of the latest techniques in working with your child's disability. Most homeschoolers are not LD, so although there are support groups, computer software, prepackaged curricula and online programs, they are not necessarily for the child with LD. Only after you have researched and exhausted all leads on homeschooling can you make a rational decision.

In a Nutshell . . .

–   Home schooling is not for every parent nor every child.
    Evaluate and research YOUR situation – do what you feel
    is best for your child.
–   Through homeschooling, parents will realize immediately
    whether or not their child is learning and understanding
    what is being taught.
–   As a parent/teacher, you have the flexibility to change
    your teaching style to match your child's learning style.
–   Always contact your State's Department of Education re-
    garding laws governing homeschooling in your state.

Frequently Asked Questions
Concerning Homeschooling

*I am thinking of trying to homeschool my daughter but
I am not sure if it is legal to do so in my state. How can
I find out without calling my local school board?*

Each state sets its own laws governing home education. Meeting the requirements of these laws may be as simple as in-
forming the school district of your intent. The best way to
find out is to call your state Department of Education.

*I don't know whether or not I have the time to home-
school my son? How much time does it take?*

Homeschooling definitely requires a time commitment but
probably not as much as you would think, since one-on-one
tutoring is more efficient than classroom instruction and, thus,
takes less time. However, please do not think that you can

homeschool in addition to holding down a full or part-time job. If you homeschool, that will be your job, your career. If you and your family need your paycheck, then you may want to rethink homeschooling.

I am homeschooling my eight-year-old daughter, and we live in an area of mostly retirees, so she does not have too many kids her age to play with. Where can I find socialization activities for her age group?

Easy question. There are literally hundreds of ways to find social opportunities for your daughter. You can schedule social opportunities with your child's peers after school, on weekends, at church, dance classes, gymnastics classes, horseback riding lessons, just to name a few. Also check with local support groups for homeschoolers; they can offer many more suggestions.

How can I learn more about the homeschooling opportunities in my state and outside of this country?

See the list below for your particular state:

ALABAMA
Christian Home Education Fellowship of Alabama, P.O. Box 563, Alabaster, AL 35007, phone (205) 664-2232

ALASKA
Alaska Private & Home Educators Association, P.O. Box 141764, Anchorage, AK 99514, phone (907) 753-3018

ARIZONA
Arizona Families for Home Education, P.O. Box 4661,

Scottsdale, AZ 85261-4661, phone (602) 443-0612

Christian Home Educators of Arizona, P.O. Box 13445, Scottsdale, AZ 85267-3445

Flagstaff Home Educators, 6910 West Suzette Lane, Flagstaff, AZ 86001-8220, phone (520) 774-0806

ARKANSAS
Arkansas Christian Home Education Association, Box 4410, North Little Rock, AR 72116, phone (501)758-9099

CALIFORNIA
Christian Home Educators Association, P.O. Box 2009, Norwalk, CA 90651, phones (310) 864-2432 or (800) 564-CHEA

Family Protection Ministries, 910 Sunrise Avenue Suite A-1, Roseville, CA 95661

COLORADO
Christian Home Educators of Colorado, 3739 East 4th Avenue, Denver, CO 80206

Concerned Parents for Colorado, P.O. Box 547, Florissant, CO 80902

CONNECTICUT
The Education Association of Christian Homeschoolers, 25 Fieldstone Run, Farmington, CT 06032

DELAWARE
Delaware Home Education Association, P.O. Box 1003, Do-

ver, DE 19003, phone (302) 698-0447

DISTRICT OF COLUMBIA
Bolling Area Home Schoolers of D.C., 1516 E. Carswell Circle, Washington, DC 20336

FLORIDA
Florida Parent-Educators Association, 3781 S.W. 18th Street, Ft. Lauderdale, FL, phone (407) 723-1714

Florida Coalition of Christian Private School Administrators, 5813 Papaya Dr., Ft. Pierce, FL 34982, phone (407) 465-1685

GEORGIA
Georgia Home Education Association, 245 Buckeye Lane, Fayetteville, GA 30214, phone (404) 461-3657

North Georgia Home Education Association, 200 West Crest Road, Rossville, GA 30741

Georgia for Freedom in Education, 209 Cobb Street, Palmetto, GA 30268, phone (404) 463-3719

HAWAII
Christian Homeschoolers of Hawaii, 91824 Oama St., Ewa Beach, HI 96706, phone (808) 689-6398

IDAHO
Idaho Home Educators, Box 4022, Boise, ID 83711, phone (208) 323-0230

ILLINOIS
Illinois Christian Home Educators, Box 261, Zion, IL 60099,

phone (847) 670-7150

Christian Home Educators Coalition, Box 470322, Chicago, IL 60647, phone (312) 278-0673

INDIANA
Indiana Association of Home Educators, 1000 N. Madison, Suite S2, Greenwood, IN 46142, phone (317) 770-0644

IOWA
Network of Iowa Christian Home Educators, Box 158, Dexter, IA 50070, phones (515) 789-4310 or (800) 723-0438

KANSAS
Christian Home Education Confederation of Kansas, P.O. Box 3564, Shawnee Mission, KS 66203, phone (316) 945-0810

KENTUCKY
Christian Home Educators of Kentucky, 691 Howardstown Road, Hodgensville, KY 42748, phone (502)358-9270

LOUISIANA
Christian Home Educators Fellowship, P.O. Box 74292, Baton Rouge, LA 70874-4292, phone (504) 642-2059

MAINE
Homeschoolers of Maine, P.O. Box 124, Hope, ME 04847, phone (207) 763-4251

MARYLAND
Maryland Association of Christian Home Education Organizations, P.O. Box 3964, Frederick, MD 21705, phone (301) 663-3999

Christian Home Educators Network, 304 North Beechwood Ave., Catonsville, MD 21228, (410) 744-8919 or (410) 444-5465

MASSACHUSETTS
Massachusetts Homeschool Organization Homeschool Org., 15 Ohio St., Wilmington, MA 01887, phone (508) 685-1061

MICHIGAN
Information Network for Christian Homes, 4934 Cannonsburg Road, Belmont, MI 49306, phone (616) 874-5656

MINNESOTA
Minnesota Association of Christian Home Educators, P.O. Box 32308, Fridley, MN 55432-0308, phone (612) 717-9070

MISSISSIPPI
Mississippi Home Educators Association, Route 9, Box 350, Laurel, MS 39440, phone (601) 649-MHEA

MISSOURI
Missouri Association of Teaching Christian Homes, 307 E. Ash Street, #146, Columbia, MO 65201, phone (314) 443-8217

Families for Home Education, 400 E. High Point Lane, Columbia, MO 65203, phone (816) 826-9302

MONTANA
Montana Coalition of Home Schools, P.O. Box 654, Helena, MT 59624, phone (406) 587-6163

NEBRASKA
Nebraska Christian Home Educators Association, P.O. Box

57041, Lincoln, NE 68505, phone (402) 423-4297

NEVADA
Home Education and Righteous Training, P.O. Box 42262, Las
Vegas, NV 89116, phone (702) 391-7219

Northern Nevada Home Schools, P.O. Box 21323, Reno, NV
89515

NEW HAMPSHIRE
Christian Home Educators of New Hampshire, P.O. Box 961,
Manchester, NH 03105

NEW JERSEY
Education Network of Christian Homeschoolers, 120 Mayfair
Lane, Mount Laurel, NJ 08054, phone (609) 222-4283

NEW MEXICO
Christian Association of Parent Educators of New Mexico, P.O.
Box 2073, Farmington, NM 87002, phone (505) 898-3908

NEW YORK
Loving Education At Home, P.O. Box 88, Cato, NY 13033,
phone (716) 346-0939

NORTH CAROLINA
North Carolinians for Home Education, 419 N. Boylan Avenue,
Raleigh, NC 27603, phone (919) 834-6243

NORTH DAKOTA
North Dakota Home School Association, 4007 N. State Street,
Route 5, Box 9, Bismarck, ND 58501, phone (701) 223-4080

OHIO
Christian Home Educators of Ohio, P.O. Box 262, Columbus, OH 43216, phone (614) 474-3177

Home Education Action Council of Ohio, P.O. Box 24133, Huber Heights, OH 45424, phone (513)242-9226

OKLAHOMA
Christian Home Educators Fellowship of Oklahoma, P.O. Box 471363, Tulsa, OK 74147-1363, phone (918) 583-7323

Oklahoma Central Home Educators, P.O. Box 270601, Oklahoma City, OK 73137, phone (405) 521-8439

OREGON
Association Network, 2515 NE 37th, Portland, OR 97212, phone (503) 288-1285

PENNSYLVANIA
Christian Home School Association of Pennsylvania, P.O. Box 3603, York, PA 17402-0603, phone (717) 661-2428

Pennsylvania Homeschoolers, R.D. 2, Box 117, Kittanning, PA 16201, phone (412) 783-6512

RHODE ISLAND
Rhode Island Guild of Home Teachers, P.O. Box 11, Hope, RI 02831-0011, phone (401) 821-1546

SOUTH CAROLINA
South Carolina Home Educators Association, P.O. Box 612, Lexington, SC 29071, phone (803) 951-8960

South Carolina Association of Independent Home Schools, P.O. Box 2104, Irmo, SC 29063, phone (803) 551-1003

SOUTH DAKOTA
Western Dakota Christian Homeschools, HCR 74, Box 28, Murdo, SD 57559, phone (605) 669-2508

TENNESSEE
Tennessee Home Education Association, 3677 Richbriar Court, Nashville, TN 37211, phone (615) 834-3529

TEXAS
Home-Oriented Private Education for Texas, P.O. Box 59876, Dallas, TX 75229-9876, phone (214) 358-2221

Texas Home School Coalition, P.O. Box 6982, Lubbock, TX 79493, phone (806) 797-4927

North Texas Home Education Network, Box 59627, Dallas TX 75229, phone (214) 234-2366

Family Educators Alliance of South Texas, 4719 Blanco Road, San Antonio, TX 78212, phone (210) 342-4674

South East Texas Home School Association, 4950 F.M. 1960W Suite C3-87, Houston, TX 77069, phone (713) 370-8787

UTAH
Utah Christian Homeschoolers, P.O. Box 3942, Salt Lake City, UT 84110-3942, phone (801) 969-9657

VERMONT
Christian Home Educators of Vermont, 2 Webster Street, Barre,

VT 05641, phone (802) 476-8821

VIRGINIA
Home Educators Association of Virginia, P.O. Box 6745, Richmond, VA 23230-0745, phone (804) 288-1608

WASHINGTON
Washington Association of Teaching Christian Homes, N. 2904 Dora Road, Spokane, WA 99212

Washington Homeschool Organization, 18130 N. Midvale Ave. Seattle, WA 98083

WEST VIRGINIA
Christian Home Educators of West Virginia, P.O. Box 8770, South Charleston, WV 25303, phone (304) 776-4664

WISCONSIN
Wisconsin Christian Home Educators, 2307 Carmel Avenue, Racine, WI 53405, phone (414) 637-5127

WYOMING
Homeschoolers of Wyoming, 221 W. Spruce St., Rawlins, WY 82301, phone (307) 324-5553

CANADA
Alberta Home Education Association, Box 3451, Leduc, Alberta T9E6M2, phone (403) 986-4264

ENGLAND
Education Otherwise, 36 Kinross Road, Leamington Spa, Warks, ENGLAND, CV32 7EF, Tel. 0926 886.882

JAPAN
KANTO Home Educators Association, PSC 477 Box 45, FPO, AP 96306-1299

GERMANY
Eifel Area Home Schoolers, 52 SPTG/MW, UNIT 3640 Box 80, APO, AE 09126

Vema Lily, PSC 118 Box 584, APO, AE 09137, 011 49 6561 5341

NEW ZEALAND
Christian Home Schoolers of New Zealand, 4 Tawa Street, Palmerston North, New Zealand

PUERTO RICO
Christian Home Educators of the Caribbean, Palmas Del Mar Mail Service, Box 888, Suite 273, Humacao, PR00791, phone (809) 852-5284

HANDICAPPED
NATHHAN (National Handicapped Homeschoolers Association Network), 5383 Alpine Road, S.E. Olalla, WA 98359, (206)857-4257

MILITARY
Christian Home Educators on Foreign Soil, Mike & Diana Smith, 1856 CSGP, PSC2 Box 8462, APO, AE 09012

RADIO
Home Education Radio Network, P.O. Box 3338, Idaho Springs, CO 80452, (303) 567-4092

See also "Suggested Reading" for Chapter 9, pp. 277-79.

Chapter 10

Tips and Pointers for Parents

Throughout this book, I have attempted to give parents of children with LD general facts on subjects that will affect their child with LD as well as other siblings and the family in general. What I want to give you now are some tried and true techniques that will help you in raising your child with LD and help you mold your child into a healthy, happy, well-adjusted child. Not all suggestions will work with every child, so you must use your judgment. Many of these tips can be used with any child, LD or not, and the tips and pointers are presented randomly and in no particular order. If you read nothing else in this book, read this chapter!

The number one challenge for parents is keeping their child's self-esteem intact (See Chapter 2, "Self-Esteem and Social Development"). Set your child up for success by giving examples to follow and allowing the child to make some of his or her own decisions, according to age and maturity, so he or she can feel the success from making the right decisions.

No one has a perfect child or family. Even though the old cliché says the grass is always greener on the other side, you know as well as I, the grass is not always greener. Everyone has a different situation to face. Having a child with LD has its peaks and valleys just as raising any child will have good times and bad. No one has a perfect child. When your neighbors or friends or relatives brag about their child or grandchild, you can still brag about your child with LD. They are children first.

Everyone has challenges, and it is okay to struggle. We all face challenges each and everyday—in business, in school, in life. We have been taught from an early age to face our problems, but unfortunately, we were never told that it is okay to struggle in order to solve our problems. When we had our children, there was no blueprint given to us on how to raise them. So in the process of raising our children, we have had to struggle no more or less than others and that is okay, too. Anyone who has said they never had to worry or fight with their child is not telling the whole truth!

Awareness is the first step to understanding. Understanding is knowledge. Knowledge is power. With awareness, understanding, knowledge and power, you gain confidence. In a way, that is what this book is all about. I cannot stress the importance of knowing as much as you can on LD, in general, and in particular knowing as much as you can about your child's disability and understanding the extent of the disability. Know your rights under the law and teach your child to advocate for themselves. Without knowledge and without understanding, you cannot fully help your child to develop into the happy and healthy individual. Reading and understanding this book is only the first step in gaining awareness and knowledge, but do not stop here. Continue reading, questioning everything and everyone in searching for a clearer picture of your child's disability.

A team approach works best. Only when all professionals (parents, child, teacher, psychologist, counselor, physician) work together to understand your child's LD problem(s) can a successful educational plan be written and implemented. As a parent, be part of the team, and if you cannot, then ask a grandparent, friend or someone who is genuinely interested in the well-being of your child to be actively involved in setting the educational goals of your child.

Advocate for your child and teach your child to advocate. Advocating is nothing more than actively negotiating on your child's behalf. At each turning point in your child's life, look over the set of options and make a decision that is in the best interest of your child. There are options at every step, so do not think you have to accept what is presented to you. Remember, keep questioning and keep probing, for there is help out there.

The only consistency is the inconsistency in dealing with progress and performance of your child. Structure is key here. Do not let the child gain control of the situation. Structure all tasks and give the commands. Your child may use many methods to avoid a given task, but stop these actions and remain task oriented. If the child has a temper tantrum, allow the child to blow off steam while you remain calm, and then let the child return to the task.

Patience, persistence and passion are a must for survival. Be firm but gentle. Speak slowly, firmly, and clearly, but never with anger or impatience. Make commands short, simple and related to the task at hand. Wait until after the command is given, then allow the child time to think it through. Remember these children must collect the facts, think them through and correlate the facts before they can perform. Above all else, give your child with LD the love and attention that all children crave.

Learning that your child is LD is sometimes hard to accept. Grieving is part of the acceptance process so take that time and remember it is not YOUR fault. It is no one's fault! Once you accept the LD problem and begin a plan of action, you will find ways to success along the way. It will not be easy, but you are not alone. Support groups are available (see Chapter 4, "The Role of the Family"), and you should share your problems with friends and family. Do not be embarrassed – there are so many other parents who have children with LD. You are not alone!

Make sure other siblings are not suffering from all the attention given that special child. Your child with LD is not the only one in the family. One child should not be allowed to disrupt families just because he or she is LD. LD is not a license which can be used to wreck havoc or destroy a family. Fine tune family activities so that all members can enjoy them and can participate. Do not be afraid to get professional help that all of you may need if the problems begin to engulf the family.

Be sure that both parents are on the same wavelength when dealing with your child with LD. Children are high management, and there are decisions around every corner, so make sure both parents agree to support and understand each other's decisions. Work as a team to create plans and implement solutions.

Medications can work wonders for ADD/ADHD children when monitored properly (see Chapter 6, "ADD and ADHD"). Keep a close eye on what drugs are used; give it time to work. As children grow, so do dosages and problems so keep a close watch over the medication. If the medication is not working, ask for other choices. Remember, keep questioning; keep probing; and keep your options open!

Learn to be a teacher – objective and impersonal – when working with your child. After the work session, go back to being the mother or father. Each parent should work with the child but not at the same time unless an additional pair of hands is needed. If both parents are working together on a project with your child, be on the same "page" so as not to confuse the child about the tasks at hand.

Children with LD are bright and creative. They are not dumb, lazy or stupid. There is only a gap between performance and ability so do not allow your child with LD to get away with murder! They can understand commands and instruction. Learn to anticipate the child's abortive and resistive moves. Draw the child's eyes into the task repeatedly. If the task proves to be too difficult, change to a simpler task and then go back to the original task. Do not abandon the first task; just find a simpler approach. A general rule of thumb is to have the child repeat what you said to make sure he or she interpreted correctly the message.

Keep choices simple and to a minimum, but above all else, do not give the child a choice unless you intend to abide by the choice. Do not use threats or promises which are only proposed actions or events that will take place at a later date. If your child is quite young or immature, threats and promises will have very little, if any, consequence as children with LD have no concept of time.

Keep in touch with your state legislators, state officials (state DOE) and try to create a partnership of private-public school funding. School choice and school vouchers are today's hot topics in state houses across our nation. Stay on top of state and local issues so that you can best prepare yourself to find the right school for your child. Lobby your state representatives! You elected them so make sure they understand what type of education you want not only for your child but for all children.

Set aside specific work periods so your child will know that NOW we perform THESE tasks. Start with short work periods – 15-30 minutes in length. Depending on your child's age, interest and aptitude, and as you gain confidence in your ability as a teacher/parent, increase the time allotment.

Use a polite, authoritative and confident voice. Develop confidence in yourself and let your voice carry this confidence to the child. Insist that the child follow each task to its completion and perform it in a manner you prescribe. However, if the child is struggling, help the child find another way to succeed. Do not allow your child to end a task unless it is completed, even if it means that you must spend extra time in helping your child find a way to achieve and succeed.

If you feel the child is ready to perform, but he or she seems unable to pull out the action, say in your authoritative and confident voice *"now"* or *"do this now."* If necessary, place your child bodily into the task. If you give a choice between two tasks, make sure the plus value of your preferred task is higher and that you make the child do the other task at another time.

Do not drill. You did not like it as a child so do not do it to your child. The initial performance is the most important. If the child puts his heart and soul into the initial performance, but it is not up to your expectations DO NOT repeat the performance more than two or three times. Praise the initial performance; leave the activity; go to another, and then return to repeat the initial performance.

Use the word *no* sparingly. Do not say *no* unless you intend to carry through and see to it that the child obeys. If you say *no*, mean *no* and if you say *no* today, make sure that the same action will bring *no* tomorrow, next week, next month, next year.

Remember that mistakes do not equal *failure*. Your child will have the tendency to see his or her mistakes as huge failures. By showing your child that you have made mistakes and have accepted your mistakes, mistakes can be useful. They can lead to new solutions. They are not the end of the world. When your child sees you taking this approach to mistakes – your own and the mistakes of others – he or she can learn to view his or her mistakes in the same light.

Allow your child to learn from their mistakes or failures to do what he or she is told. For example, leaving their bike behind a parked car in the driveway may result in the car backing over the bike, or leaving toys out in the yard near the street may result in the toys being stolen.

Recognize there may be some things your child will not be able to do or will have lifelong trouble doing. Help your child to understand that this does not mean he or she is a failure. After all, everyone has something he or she cannot do and give examples of things that are difficult for you to do. Capitalize on the things your child *can* do.

Use television creatively. Television, or videos, can be a good medium for learning. If the child is helped by using them properly, it is not a waste of time. For example, your child can learn to focus, sustain attention, listen carefully, increase vocabulary and see how the parts fit together to make a whole. You can augment learning by asking questions about what was seen: "What happened first? Then what happened? How did the story end?" Such questions encourage learning of sequence, an area that causes trouble for many children with LD. Be patient, though, because your child does not see or interpret the world in the same way you do; progress may be slow.

Encourage your child to develop his or her special talents. In what area or areas does your child excel? What does he or she especially enjoy? This goes for inside and outside the classroom. If your child enjoys swimming, encourage it or if he or she excels at dance, then encourage that. Encouraging your child to pursue areas of talent lets him or her experience success and discover a place to shine.

Teach through your child's area of strength. For example, he or she may have great difficulty reading for information but readily understand when listening. Take advantage of the strength. Rather than force reading, which will present your child with a "failure" situation, let your child learn new information by listening to a book on tape or watching a videotape.

Respect and challenge your child's natural intelligence. He or she may have trouble reading or writing, but that does not mean learning cannot take place in many other ways. Most children with learning disabilities have average or above average intelligence that can be engaged and challenged through using a multisensory approach. Taste, touch, seeing, hearing and moving are valuable ways of gathering information.

Parents must try to understand the nature of their child's problems. Like classroom teachers, they must build on the child's strengths while compensating for or adjusting to the weaknesses without exposing them unnecessarily. A child might find it hard to load a dishwasher but could carry out the trash. The same child might have difficulty catching or throwing a ball but no trouble swimming. Parents must think ahead about these matters to minimize their child's stress and to maximize their child's chance to experience success, make friends, and develop self-esteem. Treatment that affects only schoolwork will not succeed because LDs are lifelong disabilities.

Have your child look directly at you while giving a command. If you do not have your child's wholehearted attention, the command will get lost. If necessary, have your child repeat the command so that the child thoroughly understands what you want done and when.

Establish a routine for your child to follow each day. The time to get up for school, time for breakfast, a time set aside for homework as well as a time set aside for play and for chores. Stick to the routine even if it means that you need to rearrange your own schedule. Remember, children with LD and especially ADD/ADHD need structure and structure means routines.

For help in short-term memory skills, have your child recall three or four things that he or she did during the day. Do not let them off the hook by saying they did "nothing." As your child matures, increase the number of activities.

Be familiar with the school district policy on homework. For example 15 minutes for grades 1-3, 30 minutes for 4-6 grades. If your child is receiving more homework than what the district requires, then talk with your child's teacher. Homework should be a form of practice for what your child has already learned. You should not have to sit down with your child to teach him what he has already been taught. If that is the case, it may be time for a parent/teacher conference.

Spend some one-on-one time with each of your children and spend it doing something that you both like to do. Do not associate one-on-one time with homework. Allow your child to open up to you their feelings and share with them your feelings.

Get to know your child's friends and their families. Getting to know your child's friends may avoid problems later in life. Your child may have problems making friends and, therefore, will rely on the ones they have known for a long time and may not be suitable for them. If you do not like the friends, then try to find friends for your child possible through church and support groups. Remember, just because your child "runs around" with the "best families in town" does not mean their children are suitable friends with your child. Know the child as well as the family.

Do not become upset or angry when your child does something wrong. Help your child understand what he or she is doing wrong by talking calmly about the problem. If you get angry, your child will try to make excuses for the behavior.

Children with LD, ADD and/or ADHD are often the target for friendly (and even unfriendly) teasing. One of the hardest things to teach your child is how to deal and respond to friendly teasing (laughing, tease in return, avoid those individuals who do the teasing, walk away for the situation, move to another location). Explain to your child that much of the friendly teasing is a positive means by which people show others that they like them and enjoy their company. Impress upon your child that "friendly teasing" is a part of having "friends."

Teach your child what to do when he or she becomes frustrated, such as counting to 10, saying the alphabet, and better yet — leaving the situation. Do not let your child have his or her way when he or she becomes frustrated. Help him or her work through the situation.

Encourage your child to use problem-solving skills: identify the problem, identify goals and objectives, develop strategies, develop a plan for action and carry out the plan. This also helps keep the frustration level intact.

Show your child how to finish one activity before moving to another such as putting away materials before starting another activity. The earlier you teach this the better.

Computers are a wonderful invention and a godsend for the child with LD and/or ADD/ADHD. However, as with any investment of time or money, determine what your child's needs are and if you have the time and knowledge to work with your child to understand that technology, such as the use of a computer or word processor. Do not buy these items if there is no one for your child to turn to for help. This will only frustrate your child.

Use contracts as a strategy to help your child increase a skill or decrease an inappropriate behavior or for any other reason that comes to mind. The contract should be signed and agreed upon by both the child and the parent and represent: who is involved, what is expected, how the child will or can earn the expected reward and time allowed for completion of the task (See Appendix B, "Sample Contract", for an example of a contract).

Remember that rewards can be as simple as a hug or a pat on the back or extra time playing or watching television. They can also be more materialistic. But by no means make each reward bigger or better than the first reward! A simple "thank you for a job well done" can mean just as much as a materialistic gift. Today you can buy stickers to give out or you can get a little creative and make certificates on the computer. Rule of thumb – simple is better.

Written schedules tacked on the door of the child's room are helpful. They can be organized into "before" an "after" categories, e.g., "*Before* you go to school in the morning, be sure you have made your bed and hung up your clothes. Don't forget your lunch and homework." If your child does not read yet, these lists of things to do and when to do them can be read to him or her at frequent intervals.

Find out where in your community you can get a thorough evaluation on your child – educationally, psychologically, visually, neurologically, medically — and insist that the results be clearly explained to you. Also find out what special resources are available within your local school district. Whether your child is enrolled in special education in your school district or not make an appointment with the director of special education to find out what services are available. If your child is enrolled in special education, express your concerns and commitment to the education of your child.

Teach the child to relax. Depending on the age of the child, you might try to have the child practice sitting, lying, and standing perfectly still and relaxed, using a short period of time – 30 to 60 seconds. Gradually increase the time. Massage the child's neck and shoulders during this period or other times when the child seems tense. If the child seems tense when faced with a task, stop the task for a break but return to the task after the break

One more thing – parents must learn to relax, too. Be good to yourself. In our hectic lives, stress is a daily component, and you can easily double that stress if you have a child with LD. Learn to relax so you can enjoy watching your child grow and learn.

Finally, you do NOT have an LD child or an ADD/ADHD child. You have a child with LD. You have a child with ADD. You have a child with ADHD. Remember, they are children *first*.

These tips and pointers should help you relate to the LD problems that can be created if you allow them in your home. If problems persist, get professional help not only for your child, but maybe the entire family. LD is a lifelong disability, but you can help your child achieve a fulfilling life if you fully understand what you are up against.

This book is just the first step in learning about LD. Reading it shows that you do want to learn all you can about LD and that you want to help your child. You are doing yourself a favor in the long run if you, your spouse and your child work as a team to work out a plan, a strategy and a road map to help your child achieve in life.

See also "Suggested Reading" for Chapter 10, pp. 280.

Epilog

Throughout this book I have made reference to my son Dan who is LD. Today, I am happy to report that Dan is in his senior year in high school. Dan was once a shy, uncommunicative kid who at age nine could not read (1.3 reading level) and was a third-grade math student. Today he is a talkative, personable 19-year-old who has his self-esteem intact and can now read just about any book he wants to. Although his vocabulary is still weak, Dan did complete algebra I and geometry.

As Dan closes out his high school years, we are closing another chapter in his life. When we sent him off to boarding school as a shy nine-year-old, we never thought college was possible, much less graduating from high school! With the aid of our educational consultant, we have now found the right match between student and college. Whether Dan finishes college or not will be another chapter. No doubt Dan will continue to face challenges throughout his life, but now his desire to succeed, to try new opportunities and to work to the best of his ability will help him to pave the road to happiness. "Happiness." Isn't that what we all want for our children?

Appendix A

Section 504 of the Rehabilitation Act of 1973

Nondiscrimination Under Federal Grants and Programs

Sec. 504. (a) No otherwise qualified individual with a disability in the United States, as defined in section 7(8), shall, solely by reason of her or his disability, be excluded from the participation in, be denied the benefits of, or be subjected to discrimination under any program or activity receiving Federal financial assistance or under any program or activity conducted by any Executive agency or by the United States Postal Service. The head of each such agency shall promulgate such regulations as may be necessary to carry out the amendments to this section made by the Rehabilitation, Comprehensive Services, and Developmental Disabilities Act of 1978. Copies of any proposed regulation shall be submitted to appropriate authorizing committees of the Congress, and such regulation may take effect no earlier than the thirtieth day after the date on which such regulation is so submitted to such committees. (b) For the purposes of this section, the term "program" or "activity" means all of the operations of—

(1)(A) A department, agency, special purpose district, or other instrumentality of a State or a local government; or

(B) The entity of such State or local government that distributes such assistance and each such department or agency (and each other State or local government entity) to which the assistance is extended, in the case of assistance to a State or local government;

(2)(A) A college, university, or other postsecondary institution, or a public system of higher education; or

(B) A local educational agency (as defined in section 14101 of the Elementary and Secondary Education Act of 1965), system of vocational education, or other school system;

(3)(A) An entire corporation, partnership, or other private organization, or an entire sole proprietorship—

(i) If assistance is extended to such corporation, partnership, private organization, or sole proprietorship as a whole; or

(ii) Which is principally engaged in the business of providing education, health care, housing, social services, or parks and recreation; or

(B) The entire plant or other comparable, geographically separate facility to which Federal financial assistance is extended, in the case of any other corporation, partnership, private organization, or sole proprietorship; or

(4) Any other entity which is established by two or more of the entities described in paragraph (1), (2), or (3); any

part of which is extended Federal financial assistance.

(C) Small providers are not required by subsection (a) to make significant structural alterations to their existing facilities for the purpose of assuring program accessibility, if alternative means of providing the services are available. The terms used in this subsection shall be construed with reference to the regulations existing on the date of the enactment of this subsection.

(D) The standards used to determine whether this section has been violated in a complaint alleging employment discrimination under this section shall be the standards applied under title I of the Americans with Disabilities Act of 1990 (42 U.S.C. 12111 et seq.) and the provisions of sections 501 through 504, and 510, of the Americans with Disabilities Act of 1990 (42 U.S.C. 12201-12204 and 12210), as such sections relate to employment.

(29 U.S.C. 794)

Appendix B

Sample Contract

_____Agrees to:
_____
_____
_____

Expectation: _____
_____
_____

Completion Date: _____

Award: _____

Appendix C

Cost Estimates for Public, Private and Homeschooling

	PUBLIC	PRIVATE	HOME
Basic Academic Expenses			
Tuition	____	____	____
Books	____	____	____
Supplies	____	____	____
Tutoring	____	____	____
Speech therapy	____	____	____
Physical therapy	____	____	____
Occupational therapy	____	____	____
Testing	____	____	____

continued on the next page

	PUBLIC	PRIVATE	HOME

Extracurricular Activities

Music lessons/rentals	_____	_____	_____
Sports equipment	_____	_____	_____
Academic tutoring	_____	_____	_____
Art lessons	_____	_____	_____
Field trips	_____	_____	_____

Technology

| Computer hardware | _____ | _____ | _____ |
| Computer software | _____ | _____ | _____ |

Practical Expenses

Lunches/snacks	_____	_____	_____
Clothing/uniforms	_____	_____	_____
Day care	_____	_____	_____
Car and mileage	_____	_____	_____

Other Expenses _____ _____ _____

TOTAL: _____ _____ _____

Appendix D

Compensatory Techniques and Curriculum Adaptations

(reprinted by permission from
LDA Membership Application, 1997)

For Specific Learning Disabilities

While the majority of your child's educational program should be as closely aligned with the school and classroom core curriculum, there are some modifications and accommodations that can be made within a classroom *WITHOUT* upsetting the entire class. Listed below are a few such suggestions:

1.   If your child has **difficulty reading**, or is a **very slow reader**, the "read along technique" with taped textbooks

and workbooks might be used in the classroom, at home and in the resource room.

2. If your child has **memory problems**, or is unable to take notes in the classroom, a classmate might share notes by using carbon paper, or the teacher could provide a copy of the class lesson or allow your child to tape-record lessons.

3. Educational film strips and videos are available on most subjects and most grade levels for general information not acquired from the printed page. Talking books may be acquired from your local library which may also help.

4. If your child has **short term memory problems** – i.e., do not remember mathematical facts, but understand the computation process – a table of math facts and other visual aids, and a printing calculator could be provided.

5. For the child who has **difficulty writing**, a battery cassette recorder to dictate answers to tests or written lessons could be provided.

6. If your child **cannot write legibly, reverses letters, numbers or symbols** (e.g., + for x), keyboarding could be taught, the earlier the better. Each keyboard lesson is also a lesson in punctuation, spelling and vocabulary.

7. Make sure the teacher either types or uses a word processor for handouts. Also, some children may benefit from large print, or colored plastic overlays which enhances symbols and gives depth to printed page.

8. Sometimes, the use of poetry, rhymes, songs, and spell-

ing tapes will help to train memory and listening skills.

9. Spelling should be taught with a multisensory approach (say the word, spell the word orally, then write the word).

10. **Reading:** First of all, your child should be tested for ability to learn and use phonics. A child who cannot profit from phonics might be taught by alternate methods. A need for individual evaluation is indicated and make sure you ask for an evaluation if you have the slightest hint there is a problem with his or her reading. The teacher should explore different methods until a technique is found that benefits your child. Phonics is only one way to learn to read. There are other ways. Assessment should be made for instructional level as well as comprehension level. The use of flash cards for concrete words such as nouns, verbs and certain adjectives and adverbs might be helpful. Both the word and illustration of the word can be used on the flash card. Abstract words that cannot be illustrated (e.g., *of, is, if, to,* etc.) could be taught as part of a phrase or sentence on flash cards. These abstract words should be **highlighted** in the textbook. There are books available just on learning to read that may be helpful for you to review, and share some of that information from the book with your child's classroom teacher.

11. Vocabulary enrichment of content material: Your child can prepare files of vocabulary words used in a story or textbook, add definitions, write new sentences using the words, and keep them in alphabetical order. Also, large print-picture dictionaries are available for different reading levels.

12. Supplemental educational materials include:
    Large type copies of *Readers Digest* magazine and Condensed Books (many are already on tape —e.g., "Talking Tapes").
    Picture magazines: *Life*, *People*, etc.
    Maps in dark outline, color coded, large lettering.

13. **Writing:** For problems in copying, worksheets which leave space under each word, phrase or sentence for copying provide support for additional practice. Put lists of words on the right margin for left-handed students, or those with mixed- dominance (switch hitters). Ask your child's teacher to give hand-outs at the desk if your child has difficulty copying from blackboard or take dictation.

14. If your child has difficulty with **processing auditory input, (fully** understanding questions asked, recalling or forming an appropriate answer), ask your child's teacher to be patient — wait for the answer or present the question in written form.

Make sure your child is taught oral language simultaneously with written language. When reading with your child at home, have your child talk about the illustrations in the reading book which should duplicate what is read in the printed text. Watching television can also serve the same purpose.

As you can see, just a few modifications can make the world of difference in helping your child to learn and enjoy school more.

Appendix E

IDEA Amendments of 1997

On June 4, 1997, President Clinton signed into law an updated revision of PL 94-142, the Education for All Handicapped Children Act (now IDEA), which was originally enacted in 1975. The IDEA Amendments of 1997 (HR 5, S 717) restructures IDEA and divides it into four parts: Parts A (Definitions) and B (Assistance for Education of All Children with Disabilities) are permanently authorized. Parts C (Infants and Toddlers with Disabilities) and D (National Activities to Improve the Education of Children with Disabilities) are authorized for five years.

Some of the changes are significant, while others subtly fine tune the processes already laid out for schools and parents to follow in planning and providing special education and related services to children and youth with special needs. The more critically important changes include:

- participation of children and youth with disabilities in state-an district-wide assessment programs, such as SATs, state-wide testing, etc.;
- development and review of the IEP, including increased emphasis upon participation in the general education classroom and in the general curriculum (including extracurricular and nonacademic areas), with appropriate aids and services;
- parent participation in eligibility and placement decisions;
- the way in which reevaluations are conducted;
- the addition of transition planning;
- voluntary mediation as a means of resolving parent-school controversies; and
- discipline and behavior issues.

The text of HR 5 S 717, now IDEA Amendments of 1997, is printed in the May 13, 1997, Congressional Record, which may be available in your local public library. It can also be electronically downloaded from www.gov/eeo/ideadraft.htm or www.cec.sped.org/pp/idea-.htm. You can also request printed copies by faxing a request to the Senate Labor and Human Resources Committee at (202) 228-2815. Additionally, contact your U.S. Senator and/or Congressman for a copy or for a CD-ROM (there is a negligible fee) of all United States Codes, which will include IDEA. Contact:

Superintendent of Documents
Mail List Branch
Mail Stop: SSOM
Washington, DC   20401-9374

Glossary

Commonly Used Words and Phrases for LD, ADD, ADHD, Special Education Evaluations and Team Meetings

Abstract thinking — Ability to think in terms of ideas.

Advocate – A person who can help you through the special education maze and can help protect your rights. You might hire a professional advocate if you disagree with the findings of the school system and want a program for your child that is different from the one the school is offering. Often other parents who are more familiar with the special education system might be willing to accompany you to meetings and function in the role of advocate.

Agraphia – Inability to write words.

Annual Review – A yearly meeting to evaluate the effectiveness of a special education program and to determine whether it continues to work or if it should be modified.

Aphasia — Defect in or loss of the power of expression by speech, by writing, by signs, or by loss of comprehension of spoken or written language due to injury or disease of the brain centers.

Appeal – A legal process in which you request a hearing when you have a disagreement with the school system over your child's educational plan.

Articulation – The production of speech sounds and words.

Assessment – A test to determine the need for special education services.

Attention Deficit Disorder (ADD) – An inability to maintain focus and attention on a task.

Attention span – The amount of time a child can stay with a certain task.

Behavior – A set relationship between a stimulus and a response.

Behavior modification – A technique used to encourage positive actions through rewards and to discourage negative actions by ignoring them.

Bilateral – Working-togetherness of both sides of the body.

Central visual acuity – Visual faculty of perceiving the shape or form of objects in the direct line of vision.

Child study team (CST) – A pre-referral team that develops classroom modifications in an effort to prevent the necessity of a special education evaluation.

Classification – A label necessary in many states for a child to receive special education services.

Cognitive ability – A child's capacity for learning, which is related to his or her level of intelligence.

Communication – The ability to pass information to another person, either by speaking or writing or through gestures and body language.

Cylert – The trade name of one of several stimulant-type drugs used to modify hyperactivity.

Decoding – Refers to intake of verbal symbols through auditory and/or visual pathways.

Deficit – An area of difficulty that interferes with a child's learning.

Development – Interaction between maturational processes and environmental influences.

Dexedrine – The trade name of one of several stimulant-type drugs used to modify hyperactivity.

Discrepancy – A significant difference or inconsistency.

Discrimination – The ability to differentiate between two visual, auditory, kinesthetic or other sensory stimuli.

Distractibility – The inability to attend to a task due to noises, sights or thoughts.

Dyscalculia – Extreme difficulty in performing math skills.

Dysgraphia – Extreme difficulty in writing.

Dyslexia – Extreme difficulty in learning to read. Disability in making sense of printed symbols; may be due to neurological, constitutional, genetic or developmental factors.

Early intervention – The identification and education of a preschool child (before the age of three) who has a handicapping condition or is at risk of developing a handicapping condition.

Evaluation – A group of tests that determines the way in which a child learns best.

Expressive language – The ability to communicate with others by speaking, writing and/or gestures.

Fine motor – Use of generally small muscle groups for specific, fine tasks, such as speech, eye movement, or figure activities.

Free appropriate public education – As defined by the United States Public Law 94-142, it means "special education and related services which are provided at public expense, under public supervision and direction and without charge . . . and are provided in conformity with an individualized education program." In other words, a child must be educated in a way that takes into account his special learning needs, at no cost to his or her parents.

Hyperactivity – Excessive and almost constant motion that impairs a child's ability to learn.

Impulsivity – The tendency to act or speak quickly without thinking about the meaning or consequences of such actions or words.

Independent evaluation – Additional testing conducted by one or more qualified examiners not employed by the school system, identical to the type of testing done by the school. This type of testing is done when parents disagree with recommendations made by the school evaluators, or when they desire a second opinion.

Individualized Education Plan (IEP) – The document prepared by an evaluation team that details strengths and weaknesses and the specific areas in which a student will receive special help.

Integration – Working togetherness of the body.

Intervention – Most frequently, remedial treatment.

Kinesthetic – Involving muscular responses and sense of touch. Kinesthetic approaches to learning include teaching a child pre-reading skills with sandpaper letters that he or she can trace with his or her fingers.

Learning disability – A disorder in one or more of the educational processes that causes extreme difficulty in listening, thinking, speaking, reading, writing, spelling and/or calculating.

Least restrictive environment (LRE) – An educational program that allows a child to be educated, to the greatest extent possible, with students who do not need special education services.

Mainstreaming – The inclusion of special education students in regular education classes. This may involve having them participate in only art, music and/or gym classes, or may include having them in academic classes as well. See "least restrictive environment."

Modality – The way in which information is taken in by a child's senses. Specialists often refer to the visual, auditory or kinesthetic modalities and make determinations as to which modality (sight, sound, touch) is a strength or weakness for a child.

Multisensory – The use of more than one sense (sight, sound, or touch) to obtain information.

Profile – The section of an educational plan that states a student's specific strengths and weaknesses, any physical constraints, how she receives and expresses information, his or her current performance level, and other information relevant to her unique learning style.

Public Law (PL) 94-142 – The Federal law that requires each state to provide a free and appropriate education to children with disabilities.

Reevaluation – An evaluation of a student conducted every three years while he is receiving special education services. The purpose of the reevaluation is to determine if a child is still in need of current services and if new services are necessary.

Referral – The beginning of a formal evaluation process. All children must be referred to special education (by a parent, guardian or teacher) in order for testing to begin.

Related services – Any services, in addition to special education services, necessary to ensure that a student can benefit from special education. These might include transportation, specific therapies, and medical services.

Resource room – A place outside the classroom setting where a student receives special education services.

Ritalin – The trade name of one of several stimulant-type drugs used to modify hyperactivity.

Screening – A brief look at a child by special education professionals to determine if there is a need for a full evaluation.

Sensory-motor – Relationship between sensation and movement.

Special education – Specifically designed instruction to meet the unique needs of a child if he is not able to learn in a regular classroom, or if he requires special work in addition to regular classroom activities to succeed.

Tactile – The use of touch to help a student understand concepts. He or she might need to touch sandpaper letters in order to remember them, for example.

Transposition – Confusing the order of letters in words or numerals in numbers. For example, reading "girl" as "gril" or "saw" as "was", or "325" as "523".

Visual acuity – Keenness of vision.

Visual-motor – Term generally encompassing the visual receptive and motor expressive areas plus intersensory integration.

Visual processing – Taking in, understanding, remembering and using information received through the eyes.

Visual-motor integration – A student's ability to translate what he sees into a physical action. This would apply to copying letters, numbers and objects.

Whole-word method – Word analysis without the physical separation of the word into its phonetic or structural elements.

Word-attack skills – Refers to a child's ability to analyze words by syllable and phonic elements, in order to arrive at pronunciation and meaning.

Word retrieval – The ability of a student to remember and appropriately use a specific word.

Bibliography

Barkley, Russell. *Attention Deficit Hyperactivity Disorder: A Handbook for Diagnosis and Treatment*. New York: Guilford Publications, 1998.

Bernhard, Kathleen Fullerton, Ph.D. *Work With Your disAbility*. Bothell, WA: Jaks Publishing House, 1996.

Grau, Katti. "More Students Doing Their Learning Where They Live". *Newsday* (November 20, 1995).

Harwell, Joan M. *Complete Learning Disabilities Handbook*. New York: Simon & Schuster, 1989.

Nemko, Martin, Ph.D. *How to Get Your Child a Private School Education in a Public School*. Berkeley: Ten Speed Press, 1989.

Nolting, Paul D., Ph.D. *Math and Students With Learning Disabilities: A Practical Guide to Course Substitutions*. Bradenton, FL: Academic Success Press, 1991.

Nolting, Paul D., Ph.D. *Math and the Learning Disabled Student: A Practical Guide For Accommodations*. Bradenton, FL: Academic Success Press, 1988.

Nolting, Paul D., Ph.D. *Winning at Math: Your Guide to Learning Mathematics Through Successful Study Skills*. Bradenton, FL: Academic Success Press, 1987.

Phelan, Thomas, Ph.D. *All About Attention Deficit*. Glen
    Ellyn, IL: Child Management Inc., 1993.

Ray, Brian Dr. "A Nationwide Study of Home Education". Sa-
    lem, OR: National Home Education Research Institute,
    1991.

Simon, Robin. *After the Tears*. Denver: The Children's Mu-
    seum, 1987.

Smith, Sally L. *Succeeding Against the Odds*. New York:
    Putnam Publishing Group. 1991.

_____. *Statistical Brief,* Series 96-12B, State of Florida. Talla-
    hassee, FL: Department of Education, Office of Educa-
    tion Information and Accountability Services, 1994-95.

Tuttle, Cheryl Gerson, M.Ed. and Penny Paquette. *Parenting
    a Child with a Learning Disability*. New York:
    Doubleday, 1995.

Unger, Harlow. *How to Pick a Perfect Private School*. New
    York: Facts On File, 1993.

_____. *Meeting the Needs of All Students*. Olympia, WA: Wash-
    ington State Department of Education, 1993.

Suggested Reading

Chapter 1
"Identification, Diagnosis and Acceptance"

Books

Bloom, Jill. *Help Me to Help My Child*. Boston: Little, Brown, and Company, 1990.

Greene, Lawrence J. *Learning Disabilities and Your Child*. New York: Fawcett Columbine, 1987.

Rosner, J. *Helping Children Overcome L.D.* New York: Walker and Co., 1993.

Tuttle, Cheryl Gerson, M.Ed. and Penny Paquette. *Parenting a Child with a Learning Disability*. New York: Doubleday, 1995.

Periodicals and Journal Articles

Palar, Barbara Hall. "The Invisible Handicap." *Better Homes and Gardens*. March, 1994, pages 38-40, v. 72.

Reiff, Judith C. "Bridging Home and School through Multiple Intelligence." *Childhood Education*. Spring, 1996, v. 72, n3, p. 164-67.

Shannon, L.R. "How to Improve Your Grades by Checking Your Learning Styles." *The New York Times*. May 26, 1992, p. B7.

Chapter 2
"Self-Esteem and Social Development"

Books

Bloom, Jill. *Help Me to Help My Child*. Boston: Little, Brown and Company, 1990.

Cohen-Posey, Kate. *How To Handle Bullies, Teasers and Other Meanies: A Book That Takes the Nuisance Out of Name Calling and Other Nonsense*. Highland City, FL: Rainbow Books, Inc., 1995.

Osman, Betty B. *No One to Play With*. Navato, CA: Academic Therapy Publications, 1996.

_____. *The Social Side of Learning Disabilities*. New York: Random House, 1982.

Shure, Myrna. *Raising a Thinking Child: Help Your Young Child to Resolve Everyday Conflicts and Get Along with Others*. New York: H. Holt, 1994.

Periodicals and Journals

Brody, Jane E. "How to Foster Self-esteem." *The New York Times Magazine*. April 28, 1991, p. 15.

Hales, Dianne. "Capable Kids" *Working Mother*. November, 1995, pp. 54-59.

Hales, Dianne and Jenna Schnuer. "Self-talk: A Key to Self-esteem" *Working Mother*. January, 1995, pp. 35-39.

Johnson, Louanne. "Does Your Child Fear Failure?" *Parent Magazine*. February, 1993, pp. 52-54.

Katz, Lilian G. "Your Child's Self-esteem." *Parents Magazine*. November, 1988, p. 248.

Kutner, Lawrence. "Teasing Hurts!" *Parents Magazine*. September, 1995, pp. 89-91.

Seal, Kathy. "A Dose of Self-esteem: It's Better to Empower Your Child than to Simply Praise Him. *Parents Magazine*. January, 1996, p. 121.

Shahmoon Shanok, Rebecca. "Helping Left-out Kids." *Parents Magazine*. November 1990, p. 233.

Weissbourd, Richard. "The Feel-good Trap." *The New Republic*. August 19, 1996, pp. 12-15.

Chapter 3
"The Law Is On Your Side"

Books

Latham, Peter S., J.D. and Patricia H. Latham, J.D. *Learning*

Disabilities and the Law. Washington, DC: JKL Communications, 1993.

Roberts, Joseph and Bonnie Hawks. *Legal Rights Primer for the Handicapped: In and Out of the Classroom.* Novato, CA: Academic Therapy Publications, 1980.

Periodicals and Journals

Holzberg, Carol S. "Technology in Special Education." *Technology and Learning.* February, 1995, v 15, n 5, p. 18-23 and April, 1994, pp. 18-23.

NICHCY *NEWS DIGEST* (National Information Center for Children and Youth with Disabilities) P. O. Box 1492, Washington, DC 20013.

"The End of Special Education." *The New York Times.* October 7, 1996, p. 18.

Chapter 4
"The Role of the Family"

Books

Smith, Sally. *No Easy Answers - The L.D. Child at Home and at School.* New York: Bantam Books. 1995.

Periodicals and Journals

Black, Rosemary. "Can Your Kids be Friends?" *Parents Maga-*

zine. November, 1994, pp. 174-177.

Kutner, Lawrence. "When Parents Favor One Child Over Another, That Wreaks Havoc on the Sibling Relationship." *The New York Times*. September 17, 1992, p. B6.

Larkin, Daphne. "Ain't Misbehavin'." *Parenting*. November, 1993, pp. 207-209.

Malcolm, Andrew H. "Rise in Sibling (shut up!) Strains Limits (you shut up!) of Diplomacy." *The New York Times*. August 21, 1992, p. B12.

Parello, Nancy. "Learning to be a Friend." *Working Mother*. October, 1996, pp. 74-79.

Smith, Sally. "Enabling the Learning Disabled." *Instructor*. July-August, 1993, vol. 103, no. 1, p. 88.

Chapter 5
"Testing, Record Keeping and Parent/Teacher Conferences"

Books

Compton, Carolyn, Ph.D. (1984). *A Guide to 75 Tests for Special Education*. Belmont, CA: David S. Lake Publishers, 1984.

Harwell, Joan M. *Complete Learning Disabilities Handbook*. New York: Simon & Schuster, 1989.

Nolting, Paul, D., Ph.D. *How to Reduce Test Anxiety.* Bradenton, FL: Academic Success Press, Inc., 1988.

Pierangelo, Ph.D. *The Special Education Teacher's Book of Lists.* New York: Simon & Schuster, 1995.

Periodicals and Journals

Collins, Clare. "The Teachers Conference: A Team Effort." *The New York Times.* November 24, 1994, p. 69.

Enoch, Steven W. "Better Parent-Teacher Conferences." *Education Digest.* April, 1996, p. 48.

Israeloff, Roberta. "How to Talk to Your Child's School" *Parents Magazine.* October, 1992, pp. 115-119.

Seal, Kathy. "Make the Most of Your Parent-Teacher Conference." *Parents Magazine.* November, 1994, pp. 64-66.

Chapter 6
"ADD and ADHD"

Books

Clark, L. *SOS: Help for Parents.* Bowling Green, KY: Parents Press, 1989.

Fowler, M.C. *Maybe You Know My Kid: A Parent's Guide to Identifying, Understanding, and Helping Your Child with ADHD.* New York: Birch Lane Press, 1990.

Garber, Stephen W., Marianne Daniels Garber and Robyn Freedman Spizman. *Beyond Ritalin: Facts About Medication and Other Strategies for Helping Children, Adolescents, and Adults with Attention Deficit Disorders.* New York: Villard Books, 1996.

Hallowell, Edward M. with Thom Hartmann. *Driven to Distraction.* New York: Simon & Schuster, 1995.

Hartman, Thom. *Answers to Distraction.* New York: Pantheon Books, 1994.

Hartmann, Thom. *Attention Deficit Disorder: A Different Perception.* Lancaster, PA: Underwood-Miller, 1997.

Hallowell, Edward M. *When You Worry About the Child You Love.* New York: Simon & Schuster, 1996.

Ingersill, B. *Your Hyperactive Child.* New York: Doubleday, 1988.

Maxey, D.W. *How to Own and Operate An Attention Deficit Kid.* Roanoke and Charlottesville, VA: HADD, 1989.

Taylor, John F., Ph.D. *Helping Your Hyperactive/Attention Deficit Child.* Rocklin, CA: Prima Publications, 1990.

Chapter 7
"School Options #1: Public Schools"

Books

Directory of Facilities and Services for the Learning Disabled. Novato, CA: Academic Therapy Publications. 1996.

McEwan, Elaine. *Schooling Options: Choosing the Best for You and Your Child*. Wheaton, IL: H. Shaw Publishers. 1990.

Periodicals and Journals

Bergen, Doris. "Facilitating Friendship Development in Inclusion Classrooms." *Childhood Education*. Simmer, 1993, pp. 234-236.

Friend, Marilyn and Lynne Cook. "Inclusion." *Instructor*. November-December, 1993, pp. 53-58.

Jost, Kenneth. "Learning Disabilities: What is the Best Education for Students with Special Needs?" *CQ Journal*. December 10, 1993, pp. 53-58.

Pearce, Mary. "Inclusion: 12 Secrets to Make It Work in Your Classroom." *Instructor*. September, 1996, pp. 81-85.

Chapter 8
"School Options #2:
Private Day and Boarding Schools"

Books

Fielding, P.M. and John R. Moss. *A National Directory of Four Year Colleges, Two Year Colleges, and Post High School Training Programs for Young People with Learning Disabilities.* Partners In Publishing, 1994.

Kravets, Marybeth, M.A. and Imy F. Wax, M.S. *The K & W Guide to Colleges for the Learning Disabled.* New York: Random House, 1997.

Lipkin, Midge, Ph.D. *The Students with Schoolsearch Guide to Private Schools for Learning Disabilities.* Belmont, MA: Schoolsearch Press, 1992.

Lipkin, Midge, Ph.D. *Colleges with Programs or Services for Students with Learning Disabilities.* Belmont, Massachusetts: Schoolsearch Press, 1992.

Chapter 9
"School Options #3: Homeschooling"

Books

Beechick, Ruth. *You Can Teach Your Child Successfully.*

Arrow Press, (1993). (for grades 4-8)

Lopez, Diane. *Teaching Children, A Curriculum Guide to What Children Need to Know At Each Level Through Grade Six.* Wheaton, IL: Crossway Books, 1988.

McIntire, Deborah & Robert Windham. *Homeschooling — Answers to Questions Parents Most Often Ask.* Cypress, CA: Creative Teaching Press, 1995.

Moore, Raymond and Dorothy Moore. *The Successful Homeschool Family Handbook: A Creative & Stress-Free Approach to Homeschooling.* Nashville: Thomas Nelson, 1994.

Shackelford, Luanne and Susan White. *A Survivors Guide to Home Schooling.* Crossway Book, (1989).

Periodicals

Berry, Mike. "Homeschooling Takes Dedication Considering Homeschooling? Be Sure to Do Your Homework, and Contact Other Parents." *The Orlando Sentinel.* September 5, 1995, p. D4.

Chatter; Learning at Home. [Letter] *The New York Times* (Sep 24, 1995) : *New Jersey Weekly* Desk, 3.

Goodnough, Abby. "Kitchen-table Classrooms." *The New York Times.* September 24, 1995, p. 3.

Gray, Kitti. "Homework: More Students Doing Their Learning Where They Live." *Newsday.* November 20, 1995, p. A04.

"Home Schoolers Are Finding Interaction with Other Youngsters Through Cooperative Extracurricular Activities Such as Basketball and Music." *South Bend (IN) Tribune.* January 4, 1995, p. A1.

"Home Schooling Is Greatly Enhanced by Computer Technology." (Boise) *Idaho Statesman.* May 15, 1995, p. 1A.

"Number of Parents Teaching Their Children at Home Has Doubled in Three Years." *Akron (OH) Beacon Journal.* September 6, 1994, p. A1, continued on p. A8.

"Teaching School at Home." *Akron* (OH) *Beacon Journal.* September 6, 1994, p. B3.

Sykes, Debbi. "Thriving Organizations Offer Help with Home Schooling." *The News & Observer.* January 23, 1995, p. B1.

Online

http://paul.spu.edu/library/second/lc.html#Home*

http://sunsite.unc.edu/cisco/schoolhouse.html

Chapter 10
"Tips and Pointers for Parents"

Books

McCarney, Stephen B., Ed.D. and Angela Marie Bauer, M.Ed. *The Parent's Guide to Learning Disabilities*. Columbia, MO: Hawthorne Education Services, Inc. 1991.

Nolting, Paul D., Ph.D. *Math and the Learning Disabled Student: A Practical Guide for Accommodations*. Bradenton, FL: Academic Success Press, Inc., 1992.

_____ . *Winning at Math: Your Guide to Learning Mathematics through Successful Study Skills*. Bradenton, FL: Academic Success Press, Inc., 1997.

Scheiber Barbara and Jeanne Talpers. *Unlocking Potential*, Bethesda, Maryland: Adler & Adler, 1987.

Online

LDA — http://www.ldanatl.org/
Exceptional Websites: Learning Disabilities — http://www.chre.vt.edu/Faculty-Staff/bbilling/links/LD.html
National Center for LD — http://www.ncld.org/
NICHCY — http://nichcy.org/
Parent Soup: Facts About LD — http://www.parentsoup.com/library/bsa040.html
LD in Depth — http://www.ldonline.org/ld_indepth/general_info/general.html
Academic Success Press — http://www.academicsuccess.com

Index

About the Author

MARY CATHRYN HALLER

Mary Cathryn Haller received a B.S. in Business (Marketing and Management) from Barry University in Miami and a Master's in Education from Georgia State University. After teaching high school in Georgia and Colorado for five years, Mrs. Haller returned to Florida to enter her family's business. After 15 years in the development business, she retired in 1994 to spend more time with her children.

As a former resident of Bradenton, FL, Mrs. Haller served on the state board of Learning Disabilities of Florida as Secretary. She was also active in her community—American Association of University Women, Charter Trustee of Century Bank, Manisota LDA, local Chamber of Commerce, gubernatorial appointment to the Board of Trustees for the John and Mable

Ringling Museum of Art, and life member of Entre Nous (a service organization). Since moving to Colorado Springs, she is a member of the Colorado Springs Chamber of Commerce, Leadership Pikes Peak, SCORE, Southern Colorado Women Chamber of Commerce, and the local chapter of NABOW.

Today, Mary Cathryn Haller resides with her husband, Greg Haller, an attorney, and they have two children: Chris, a graduate of Texas Christian University in Ft. Worth, Texas, where he lives and works, and Dan has been accepted into the Outdoor Leadership Program at Colorado Mountain College in Steamboat Springs, Colorado, for September 1999. Mrs. Haller has begun her second book — a primer for women aspiring to be entrepreneurs. Aside from writing, she enjoys golf, skiing and politics.